ORNE
BRIDGEHEAD

The 'Battle Zone Normandy' Series

Orne Bridgehead Lloyd Clark
Sword Beach Ken Ford
Juno Beach Ken Ford
Gold Beach Simon Trew
Omaha Beach Tim Bean
Utah Beach Stephen Badsey
Villers-Bocage George Forty
Battle for Cherbourg Robin Havers
Operation Epsom Lloyd Clark
Battle for St-Lô Nigel de Lee
Battle for Caen Simon Trew
Operation Cobra Christopher Pugsley
Road to Falaise Steve Hart
Falaise Pocket Paul Latawski

All of these titles can be ordered via the Sutton Publishing website www.suttonpublishing.co.uk

The 'Battle Zone Normandy' Editorial and Design Team

Series Editor Simon Trew
Senior Commissioning Editor Jonathan Falconer
Assistant Editor Nick Reynolds
Cover and Page Design Martin Latham
Editing and Layout Donald Sommerville
Mapping Map Creation Ltd
Photograph Scanning and Mapping Bow Watkinson
Index Michael Forder

BATTLE
ZONE
NORMANDY

ORNE
BRIDGEHEAD

LLOYD CLARK

Series Editor: Simon Trew

Sutton Publishing

First Published in 2004 by
Sutton Publishing Limited · Phoenix Mill
Thrupp · Stroud · Gloucestershire · GL5 2BU

Text Copyright © Lloyd Clark 2004
Tour map overlays Copyright © Sutton
Publishing
Tour base maps Copyright © Institut
Géographique National, Paris
GSGS (1944) map overlays Copyright ©
Sutton Publishing
GSGS (1944) base maps Copyright ©
The British Library/Crown Copyright

Lloyd Clark has asserted the moral right to be
identified as the author of this work.

British Library Cataloguing in Publication Data
A catalogue record for this book is available
from The British Library.

ISBN 0-7509-3009-8

While every effort has been made to ensure
that the information given in this book is
accurate, the publishers, the author and the
series editor do not accept responsibility for
any errors or omissions or for any changes in
the details given in this guide or for the
consequence of any reliance on the
information provided. The publishers would be
grateful if readers would advise them of any
inaccuracies they may encounter so these can
be considered for future editions of this book.
The inclusion of any place to stay, place to eat,
tourist attraction or other establishment in
this book does not imply an endorsement or
recommendation by the publisher, the series
editor or the author. Their details are included
for information only. Directions are for
guidance only and should be used in
conjunction with other sources of information.

Typeset in 10.5/14 pt Sabon

Printed and bound in England by
J.H. Haynes & Co. Ltd, Sparkford

Front cover: Airborne troops emplaning. *(Imperial War Museum [IWM] H39071)*

Page 1: The modern Pegasus Bridge from the east, looking across the Caen Canal. In the
foreground is a preserved German 50-mm anti-tank gun. *(Author)*

Page 3: Parachutists dropping from Douglas C-47 Skytrains. *(IWM H39684)*

Page 7: Allied troops advancing through Ste-Honorine. *(IWM B9358)*

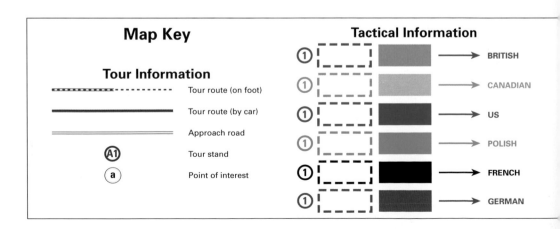

Map Key

Tour Information

········· - - - - - - - - -   Tour route (on foot)

━━━━━━━━━━━━   Tour route (by car)

═══════════════   Approach road

(A1)   Tour stand

(a)   Point of interest

Tactical Information

(1) ⌐ - - - ¬ ▭ ⟶ BRITISH

(1) ⌐ - - - ¬ ▭ ⟶ CANADIAN

(1) ⌐ - - - ¬ ▭ ⟶ US

(1) ⌐ - - - ¬ ▭ ⟶ POLISH

(1) ⌐ - - - ¬ ▭ ⟶ FRENCH

(1) ⌐ - - - ¬ ▭ ⟶ GERMAN

CONTENTS

THE NORMANDY BATTLEFIELD

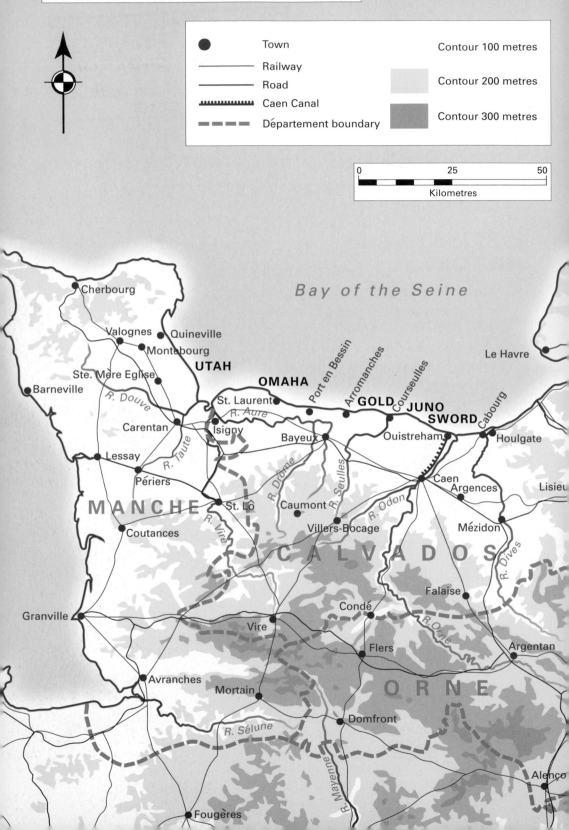

Town
Railway
Road
Caen Canal
Département boundary

Contour 100 metres
Contour 200 metres
Contour 300 metres

0   25   50
Kilometres

Bay of the Seine

Cherbourg

Valognes   Quineville
Montebourg
Ste. Mère Eglise   UTAH
Barneville   OMAHA   Port en Bessin   Arromanches   Courseulles   Le Havre
R. Douve   St. Laurent   GOLD   JUNO   Cabourg
Carentan   Isigny   R. Aure   SWORD
Lessay   R. Taute   Bayeux   Ouistreham   Houlgate
Périers   R. Drôme   R. Seulles   R. Odon   Caen   Argences   Lisieux
MANCHE   St. Lô   Caumont   Villers-Bocage   Mézidon
Coutances   R. Vire   CALVADOS   R. Dives
Falaise
Granville   Condé   R. Orne   Argentan
Vire   R. Orne
Flers
Avranches   ORNE
Mortain
R. Sélune   Domfront
R. Mayenne   Alenço
Fougères

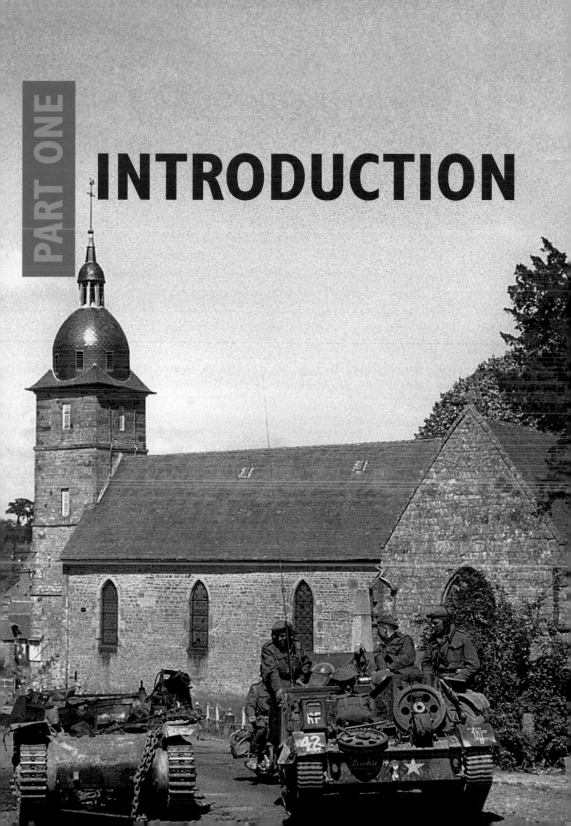

PART ONE

INTRODUCTION

BATTLE ZONE NORMANDY

The Battle of Normandy was one of the greatest military clashes of all time. From late 1943, when the Allies appointed their senior commanders and began the air operations that were such a vital preliminary to the invasion, until the end of August 1944, it pitted against one another several of the most powerful nations on earth, as well as some of their most brilliant minds. When it was won, it changed the world forever. The price was high, but for anybody who values the principles of freedom and democracy, it is difficult to conclude that it was one not worth paying.

I first visited Lower Normandy in 1994, a year after I joined the War Studies Department at the Royal Military Academy Sandhurst (RMAS). With the 50th anniversary of D-Day looming, it was decided that the British Army would be represented at several major ceremonies by one of the RMAS's officer cadet companies. It was also suggested that the cadets should visit some of the battlefields, not least to bring home to them the significance of why they were there. Thus, at the start of June 1994, I found myself as one of a small team of military and civilian directing staff flying with the cadets in a draughty and noisy Hercules transport to visit the beaches and fields of Calvados, in my case for the first time.

I was hooked. Having met some of the veterans and seen the ground over which they fought – and where many of their friends died – I was determined to go back. Fortunately, the Army encourages battlefield touring as part of its soldiers' education, and on numerous occasions since 1994 I have been privileged to return to Normandy, often to visit new sites. In the process I have learned a vast amount, both from my colleagues (several of whom are contributors to this series) and from my enthusiastic and sometimes tri-service audiences, whose professional insights and penetrating questions have frequently made me re-examine my own assumptions and prejudices. Perhaps inevitably, especially when standing in one of Normandy's beautifully-maintained Commonwealth War Graves Commission cemeteries, I have also found myself deeply moved by the critical events that took place there in the summer of 1944.

'Battle Zone Normandy' was conceived by Jonathan Falconer, Commissioning Editor at Sutton Publishing, in 2001. Why not, he suggested, bring together recent academic research – some of which challenges the general perception of what happened on and after 6 June 1944 – with a perspective based on familiarity with the ground itself? We agreed that the opportunity existed for a series that would set out to combine detailed and accurate narratives, based mostly on primary sources, with illustrated guides to the ground itself, which could be used either in the field (sometimes quite literally), or by the armchair explorer. The book in your hands is the product of that agreement.

The 'Battle Zone Normandy' series consists of 14 volumes, covering most of the major and many of the minor engagements that went together to create the Battle of Normandy. The first six books deal with the airborne and amphibious landings on 6 June 1944, and with the struggle to create the firm lodgement that was the prerequisite for eventual Allied victory. Five further volumes cover some of the critical battles that followed, as the Allies' plans unravelled and they were forced to improvise a battle very different from that originally intended. Finally, the last three titles in the series examine the fruits of the bitter attritional struggle of June and July 1944, as the Allies irrupted through the German lines or drove them back in fierce fighting. The series ends, logically enough, with the devastation of the German armed forces in the 'Falaise Pocket' in late August.

Whether you use these books while visiting Normandy, or to experience the battlefields vicariously, we hope you will find them as interesting to read as we did to research and write. Far from the inevitable victory that is sometimes represented, D-Day and the ensuing battles were full of hazards and unpredictability. Contrary to the view often expressed, had the invasion failed, it is far from certain that a second attempt could have been mounted. Remember this, and the significance of the contents of this book, not least for your life today, will be the more obvious.

Dr Simon Trew
Royal Military Academy Sandhurst
December 2003

INTRODUCTION

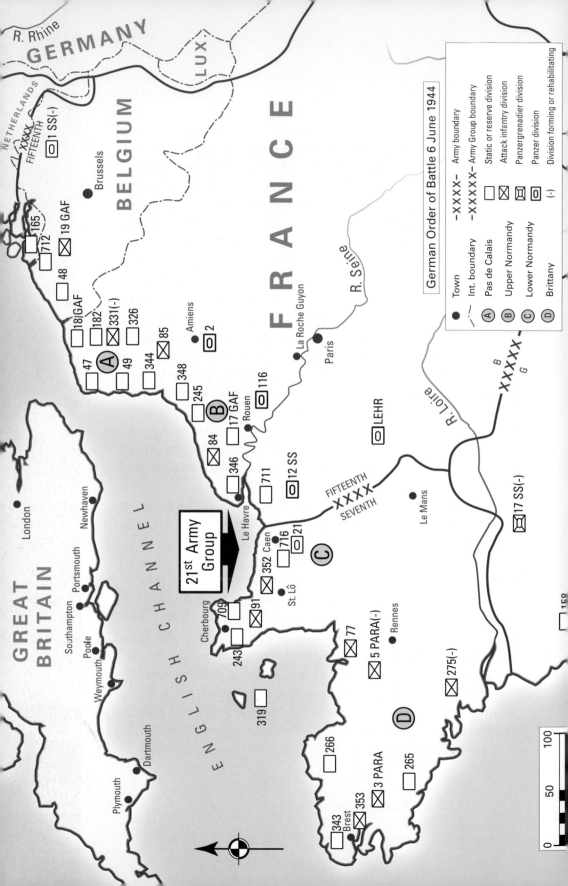

ACKNOWLEDGEMENTS

There are many people whom I must thank for the help and encouragement that they have given me during the research and writing of this book, but I must stress that any mistakes in it are mine and mine alone: the team at Sutton Publishing and particularly Jonathan Falconer and Nick Reynolds; my friend and colleague Dr Simon Trew, the series editor, who has been so helpful with sources and intoxicatingly enthusiastic about this bold project from the outset; Andrew Orgill and his staff at the Central Library, RMA Sandhurst; the staff at the National Archive, Kew; the staff at the Departments of Documents, Books and Photographs at the Imperial War Museum; Mark Worthington and the staff at the Pegasus Memorial in Normandy; the staff at the Merville Battery Museum; Neil Barber for his expertise on 9 Para; Alan Brown at the Airborne Forces Museum Aldershot; my colleagues in the Department of War Studies at RMA Sandhurst; the Airborne Assault Normandy Trust and particularly Major Jack Watson, MC; my fellow battlefield tourers based in Sussex and particularly Ro Horrocks for her forbearance, kindness and flexibility, the 'BCGs': Vanessa Gill for the use of her office and the cups of tea; Duncan Gill for our chats about bravery and remarkable exploits of derring-do; Sim and Julia 'Margo' Bowman for their insights into the minds of 12th (Yorkshire) Battalion; Mark Baldwin for his unrivalled knowledge about flying Second World War aircraft and Sarah Baldwin for her uncanny ability to find good bars and cafés. Once again, however, for their total understanding of a man obsessed with Europe at war, both during 1914–18 and 1939–45, I thank my family, Freddie, Charlotte and Henry, and my remarkably tolerant wife Catriona. This book is dedicated to her with my love.

Lloyd Clark
Royal Military Academy Sandhurst
July 2003

INTRODUCTION

PART TWO

HISTORY

HISTORY

CHAPTER I

THE DEVELOPMENT OF AIRBORNE WARFARE

This book is concerned with one of the most remarkable military operations ever, the opening of the Second Front in Normandy in the early summer of 1944. More particularly, it deals with the dramatic employment of 6th British Airborne Division on D-Day, 6 June, and its actions during the six days thereafter. There can be few episodes in military history as fascinating as that of a highly trained yet immensely vulnerable

Above: King George VI and Queen Elizabeth visiting 6th Airborne Division on 19 May 1944. The first aircraft is an Albemarle, the second a Halifax ready to tow a Hamilcar glider and the third is a Short Stirling with a Horsa glider. *(IWM CH18775)*

Page 13: The 1st Special Service Brigade passing through a French village on 6 June. The location of the photograph is not known and the fact that they are wearing berets rather than their helmets is not necessarily evidence that the enemy are some distance away. Many commandos crossed the bridge over the Caen Canal in soft headgear although it was under German fire. *(IWM B5067)* division, dropping from the sky behind enemy lines to assist in the efforts of an enormous amphibious operation to initiate an immensely important campaign. Part of the fascination with the events relating to 6th Airborne Division in Normandy in June 1944 must surely be the perceived romance of airborne operations. Airborne warfare is special in many ways, not least in its potential as a great psychological tool that can achieve the most remarkable successes, but also in its unhappy knack of spawning military disasters.

A battalion exercise during spring 1944 from RAF Douglas Dakota aircraft. The parachutists jumped from as low as 300 feet (90 m) into Normandy which gave them precious little time to orientate themselves before landing. (IWM CH13076)

Airborne warfare has always been a risky business, but whether troops during the Second World War were inserted into battle by parachute or by glider, their ability to produce paralysing speed and surprise relied not just on good equipment, first-class training and a sympathetic plan, but also required that their isolation, limited firepower and poor mobility were not exploited by an enemy who did not suffer from the same disadvantages. Such challenges may well go some way towards explaining why airborne warfare is so fascinating, but they also reveal why an airborne operation should not be considered unless the military circumstances absolutely demand it – that the airborne objectives are a critical operational requirement and there is no alternative means by which to achieve them. Historically numerous operations have not fulfilled these requirements, but the Normandy battle was not one of them.

Three airborne divisions were dropped and air-landed into Normandy on 6 June 1944, two of them American, the 82nd and 101st, on the west flank (see the companion volume in this series

General Sir Bernard Montgomery inspecting 6th Airborne Division in March 1944. Maj-Gen Richard Gale is on the far right with Brigadier James Hill peering at the containers with hands clasped together. (IWM H36426)

Parachuting in 1944

On exiting the aircraft, the soldier adopted the 'attention' position with his arms tight to his sides. The parachute would be opened automatically by the static line attached to the aircraft. There would then be some swinging in the harness underneath the parachute and this needed to be brought under control quickly as the parachutist had just seconds before landing. As well as the usual range of personal weapons and equipment a para often also carried a kit bag attached to his leg by a cord. As he descended towards the ground he would lower this beneath him so that it reached the ground first and therefore did not make his own landing unduly heavy. A safe landing could never be guaranteed, however, particularly on hard grounds and at night when the ground could not be seen. Once on the ground a parachutist then had to hope that the enemy was not in the immediate vicinity, establish whether or not he had been landed accurately and then make his way to the RV point.

Captain J.A.N. Sim, 12 Para:

'... the red, and then the green lights went on and I stepped through the hole. There was a sudden stillness, the clean crisp rush of air behind the ears and round the body, the swelling of the chute above as it developed, sensations quickly following one after another, and I found myself floating lazily down, silently and, it seemed, alone...'

Sergeant Tom Wood, 12 Para:

'There was a rush of air from the slipstream; we were on static lines and the chutes opened automatically as we dropped from about 600 feet. The anti-aircraft fire looked like fireworks, coming lazily up, and didn't look particularly dangerous; I was concentrating on getting myself right. Weapons stuck through my equipment, ammunition, explosives, a kit bag on my leg with more ammunition, which had to be released so that it landed first... I [landed in a tree but] trees can be a good landing. There was a quarter moon. I cut myself down with my fighting knife, fell and was badly bruised... Where was I? I hadn't a clue but I knew I wasn't where I should have been.'

Source: Eric Barley and Yves Fohlen, *Para Memories*.

Battle Zone Normandy: *Utah Beach*) and the British 6th on the east flank. The tasks that these divisions had to accomplish were deemed crucial to the success of the Allied invasion of Normandy (Operation 'Neptune') by the planners and General Dwight D. Eisenhower, Supreme Commander Allied Expeditionary Force and General Sir Bernard Montgomery, Commander 21st Army Group, in particular.

It was the task of 6th Airborne Division, commanded by Major-General (Maj-Gen) Richard Gale, to protect the left flank of the Allied seaborne assault from German counter-attacks by establishing a buffer zone between the Caen Canal and the River

Dives, having first seized intact key bridges across water obstacles to facilitate its own speedy reinforcement and relief. There was no possibility of extending the invasion beaches further to the east so that troops landing from the sea could take these objectives. Not only would they have been vulnerable to the guns situated at Le Havre, they would also have struggled to make their way through the hinterland around the River Dives which had been deliberately flooded by the enemy. In any case, by the time that such troops might have reached objectives some distance inland, the Germans would surely have strengthened their grip on critical ground and ensured that vital bridges were blown. The deployment of the British airborne division, however, provided an opportunity to secure vulnerable objectives before the enemy had a chance to react. Failure to take these objectives might allow the Germans to attack an exposed flank of the invasion force when it was extremely vulnerable. If successful, the airborne troops could not only protect the landings, but also provide the hinge upon which the Allied forces could then turn in order to break out from their Normandy beachhead.

This book examines the fighting that was conducted in the 6th Airborne Division area of operations from the initial landings on 6 June, through to 12 June, D+6, when the Allied left flank was finally secured.

Troops are given a final briefing before a practice jump at Netheravon in the spring of 1944. (IWM H25451)

King George and Queen Elizabeth visiting 6th Airborne Division on 19 May 1944.
Maj Gen Gale at left in front of the open nose of a Hamilcar glider. *(IWM CH13137)*

A BRIEF HISTORY OF BRITISH AIRBORNE FORCES 1940–44

Airborne warfare was still a relatively new fighting concept for the British Army in 1944, as it was to most countries at the time. However, Germany had been at the forefront of its development during the inter-war years and had then used parachutists and gliders in Holland, Belgium and Norway during the early days of the Second World War. These German operations, although far from unqualified successes, did reveal the potential of such troops. Consequently, soon after Sir Winston Churchill, the British Prime Minister, famously wrote in June 1940, 'We ought to have a corps of at least 5,000 parachute troops', the development of British airborne forces began.

The men who joined the airborne forces initially were volunteers. They tended to be men who were not afraid of something new or the sort of bold operations that such forces were likely to undertake – indeed, many were attracted by these possibilities. However, the mere desire to be an airborne soldier was not enough. Applicants had to be fit, confident, intelligent, tenacious, brave and have the desire to fight. If they passed the various tests, these men were soon bonded by the rigorous selection procedure, their special training, the badges on their arms and the maroon berets on their heads which revealed them to be amongst the best of their ilk. They were British soldiers, but they were a breed apart.

HISTORY

General Montgomery gives an informal talk to parachutists from the 6th Airborne Division in March 1944. The fact that he wore the beret presented to him by the GOC 1st Airborne Division, Maj-Gen Hopkinson, when he visited airborne troops in Sicily the previous year (and to which he was not strictly entitled), annoyed many of the fiercely proud airborne soldiers. *(IWM H36440)*

During their early days the airborne forces had to unravel a tangled skein of issues surrounding their training, planning, deployment and fighting methods. Since there was no airborne past from which to draw lessons, everything – from specialist weapons and equipment to doctrine – had to be made up as they went along. Progress was slow and the first use of these forces in February 1941 against the Tragino aqueduct in southern Italy ended in failure when all 38 paratroopers were captured. Nevertheless, faith was not lost and, on 31 August 1941, 1st Parachute Brigade was formed under Brigadier Richard Gale, consisting of 1st, 2nd, 3rd and 4th Parachute Battalions and No. 1 Air Troop, Royal Engineers. During the autumn an infantry brigade was also converted into an airlanding brigade. It was commanded by Brigadier G.F. Hopkinson and included the 2nd Battalion, Oxfordshire and Buckinghamshire Light Infantry (2 OBLI), and 1st Battalion, Royal Ulster Rifles (1 RUR).

Canadian Parachute Corps badge on the le Mesnil memorial. *(Author)*

The result of these expansions was the establishment of an airborne division, and the father of British airborne forces, Frederick 'Boy' Browning, was promoted to the rank of major-general and appointed as 'Commander Paratroops and Airborne Troops'.

Browning gave a great boost to the development of parachute and glider troops. In early 1942 the Army Air Corps was established to administer the parachute battalions and 2nd Parachute Brigade was formed. The rapid growth of parachute forces meant, however, that previously-existing infantry battalions had to be converted to the parachute role, rather than relying exclusively on volunteers; it was in this way that 5th and 6th Parachute Battalions were formed. Change was rapid and many questions were asked in both political and military circles about the need for airborne

Royal Ulster Rifles cap badge. *(Author)*

forces at a time when there were so many other calls on valuable resources. All the airborne fraternity were therefore relieved when the raid against the German radar station at Bruneval on the northern coast of France, by a company of 2nd Parachute Battalion in February 1942, was a great success. Bruneval revealed the potential worth of airborne warfare, yet resources were still scant. Even so Browning continued to oversee the development and growth of this new arm, not least in nurturing its relationship with the RAF. Before long 3rd and 4th Parachute Brigades were raised,

Order of Battle, 6th Airborne Division
June 1944

General Officer Commanding	*Maj-Gen R.N. Gale*
Divisional Headquarters	
GSOI (Ops)	*Lt-Col R.H.N.C. Bray*
GSOI (Air)	*Lt-Col W.B.P. Bradish*
AA and QMG	*Lt-Col W.S.F. Hickie*
ADMS	*Col M. MacEwan*
3rd Parachute Brigade	***Brig S.J.L. Hill***
8 Parachute Battalion	*Lt-Col A.S. Pearson*
9 Parachute Battalion	*Lt-Col T.B.H. Otway*
I Canadian Parachute Battalion	*Lt-Col G.F.P. Bradbrooke*
5th Parachute Brigade	***Brig J.H.N. Poett***
7 Parachute Battalion	*Lt-Col R.G. Pine-Coffin*
12 Parachute Battalion	*Lt-Col A.P. Johnson*
13 Parachute Battalion	*Lt-Col P.J. Luard*
22nd Independent Para Company	*Maj F. Lennox-Boyd*
6th Airlanding Brigade	***Brig The Hon H.K.M. Kindersley***
Deputy	Col R.G. Parker
12th Battalion, Devonshire Regiment	*Lt-Col R. Stevens*
2nd Battalion, Ox & Bucks Light Inf	*Lt-Col M.W. Roberts*
1st Battalion, Royal Ulster Rifles	*Lt-Col R.J.H. Carson*
Divisional Troops:	
Royal Artillery	Lt-Col J.S.L. Norris
53 Airlanding Light Regiment	*Lt-Col A.D.M. Teacher*
(210, 211 & 212 AL Light Btys)	
3 Airlanding Anti-Tank Battery	*Maj W.R. Cranmer*
4 Airlanding Anti-Tank Battery	*Maj T.H.P. Dixon*
2 Airlanding Light Anti-Aircraft Battery	*Maj W.A.H. Rowat*
2 Forward Observer Unit	*Maj H.J.B. Rice*

the former consisting of 7th, 8th and 9th Parachute Battalions commanded by Brigadier Gerald Lathbury.

Meanwhile, 1st Parachute Brigade was sent to North Africa in November 1942 where it was involved in the first Allied airborne operations of the war. This experience was crucial for the planners, commanders, officers and men for the operations that were to come, and it was here that the Parachute Regiment also first achieved its fearsome fighting reputation. The brigade returned to England in April 1943, having suffered 1,700 casualties, to be replaced by a larger force, consisting of 2nd and 4th Parachute Brigades and 1st Airlanding Brigade, which itself returned home in November after operations in Sicily.

Whilst 1st British Airborne Division was cutting its teeth in

Reconnaissance

6 Airborne Div Armd Recce Regt	Lt-Col G.R. de C. Stewart

Royal Engineers — Lt-Col F.H. Lowman

3 Parachute Squadron	Maj J.C.A. Roseveare
591 Parachute Squadron	Maj P.A. Wood
249 Field Company	Maj A.H. Rutherford
286 Field Park Company	Maj J.H. Waters

Royal Signals

6 Airborne Division Signals	Lt-Col D. Smallman-Tew

RASC — Lt-Col J.L. Watson

716 Light Composite Company	Maj A. Jones
398 Composite Company	Maj M.E. Phillips
63 Composite Company	Maj A.C. Bille-Top

RAMC

224 Parachute Field Ambulance	Lt-Col D.H. Thompson
225 Parachute Field Ambulance	Lt-Col E.I.B. Harvey
195 Airlanding Field Ambulance	Lt-Col W.M.E. Anderson

RAOC

6 Airborne Div Ordnance Field Park	Maj W.L. Taylor

REME — Lt-Col R.V. Powditch

6 Airborne Division Workshop	Maj E.B. Bunniwell

Provost Company — Capt Irwin

AAC

No. 1 Wing, Glider Pilot Regiment	Lt-Col I.A. Murray
No. 2 Wing, Glider Pilot Regiment	Lt-Col P. Griffiths

Intelligence Corps

317 Field Security Section	Capt F.G. Macmillan

North Africa, on 23 April 1943 the War Office decided that a second airborne division should be formed. This formation, designated 6th Airborne Division, was based around the 3rd Parachute Brigade, supplemented in May by the recently raised 6th Airlanding Brigade and in July by the new 5th Parachute Brigade. This latest division was to be commanded by the newly promoted Maj-Gen Gale and by early May he had established his headquarters in Syrencote House near Figheldean in Wiltshire. In one of the first copies of Divisional Routine Orders Gale decided on the divisional motto, 'Go To It!' By August 1943 the division comprised: 3rd Parachute Brigade, commanded by 31-year-old Brigadier S.J.L. Hill; 5th Parachute Brigade, commanded by Brigadier J.H.N. Poett; and 6th Airlanding Brigade which was

HISTORY

commanded by Brigadier H. Kindersley. Divisional units, it should also be remembered, were critical for the infantry to do their job, and these included reconnaissance troops, gunners, engineers, signallers, medics, supply troops, field workshops and military police. (*See order of battle on pp. 22–23.*)

A photograph taken in 1944 during instruction in parachute jumping. Here an instructor jumps through a hole in the fuselage of an Albemarle. *(IWM CH13189)*

This new division had a great deal of work to do to get itself up to operational status at a time when everybody concerned recognised that an Allied invasion of North-West Europe, in which airborne forces could well have a key role, was imminent. As a result the staff immediately began to absorb as much as they could from previous airborne operations and conducted exercises both with and without troops. The first exercise, 'Pegasus', was conducted in June 1943 and focused on the employment of the division in support of an assault on North-West Europe. It is interesting to note, bearing in mind the tasks given to 6th Airborne Division during the D-Day invasion, that in Pegasus the division assaulted a heavily defended coastal defence battery, denied the enemy ground from which they could observe the area assault operation and delayed the movement of enemy reserves into the battle area. Just before Christmas, the division was ordered to mobilise and prepare for operations by 1 February 1944.

CHAPTER 2

PREPARATION, PLANNING AND THE ENEMY

On 23 February 1944 Gale was given his orders for the invasion of Normandy and shortly afterwards his staff began detailed planning at HQ, Airborne Troops, in London. Gale was told that I Corps, with the British 3rd Infantry Division on the left, was itself to be on the left of an assault by Second (British) Army. Adjacent to 3rd Division on the left flank were the Caen Canal and the River Orne which were overlooked by a wooded ridge to the east. It was 6th Airborne Division's job to protect this eastern flank from enemy attacks and to dominate the area between the Caen Canal and the River Dives – over which certain bridges were to be destroyed – and to seize crucial bridges across the Caen Canal and River Orne intact in order to facilitate its own relief and to provide a launch pad for further Allied exploitation.

The troops available to Gale were 6th Airborne Division and 1st Special Service Brigade which, having landed over the

Maj-Gen Gale talking to airborne troops at their transit camps on 4 June 1944. Gale travelled round to each of these camps in the days immediately before the men were flown to Normandy and at one said, 'The Hun thinks only a bloody fool will go there – that's why I'm going!' *(IWM H39076)*

HISTORY

beaches, would come under his command when the troops entered the airborne division's area of operations. Nos. 38 and 46 Groups, RAF, would carry the division; even so, only two-thirds of the division could be carried in the first lift. The staff had therefore to decide which units needed to be landed first based on the priority objectives that had to seized: the taking and holding of the bridges over the Caen Canal and the River Orne; the neutralisation of the gun battery at Merville, which threatened Sword Beach; and the destruction of bridges over the River Dives at or near Troarn, Bures, Robehomme and Varaville to hinder German movement into the area from the east. Once these objectives were achieved, the high ground between the Orne and the Dives was to be consolidated and a firm base established to hold off any counter-attacks from the east and south.

8 March 1944 – General Montgomery flanked on his right by Maj-Gen Gale and his left by Brigadier The Hon H.K.M. Kindersley, commander of 6th Airlanding Brigade. Kindersley had not been a regular before the war but had won an MC in France in 1918. During the inter-war years he had been successful in the City and enjoyed flying private aircraft. He led a Churchill tank battalion of the Scots Guards before taking command of the airlanding brigade, and then qualifying as a parachutist and a glider pilot, at the grand old age of 44. *(IWM H36441)*

The German Army in the West was not, in general terms, a strong one in June 1944. After four years of occupation duties it was difficult for the veteran German Commander-in-Chief West (OB West) *Generalfeldmarschall* (Field Marshal) Gerd von Rundstedt to ensure that all his troops were sharp in spite of the likelihood of an Allied invasion in the near future. Under his command were Army Groups B and G. Army Group B (43 divisions), led by Field Marshal Erwin Rommel, was deployed on the north coast from Brittany to Antwerp. This army group included Seventh Army, led by *Generaloberst* (Colonel-General) Friedrich Dollmann and Fifteenth Army, under Col-Gen Hans von Salmuth. Seventh Army's LXXXIV Corps (6 divisions), commanded by *General der Artillerie* (General of Artillery) Erich Marcks held the area from the St-Malo estuary to the River Dives, a distance of 380 kilometres (km), from where Fifteenth Army's LXXXI Corps took over.

OB West was ordered to 'prevent any landings in its area. The main line of resistance is the high tide line on the coast. Should the enemy land at any place, they are to be immediately thrown back into the sea.' This was an easily understandable aim, but the chances of it being achieved were hampered by weaknesses in the quality of the defending troops and their defences in the 'Atlantic Wall', difficulties with command and control, and differences of opinion as to how to employ the armoured reserve.

Despite significant improvements from November 1943, by June 1944 the defending troops were still not of the highest quality. This was partly because the West had become a backwater for convalescents and those unfit for active service on the Eastern Front. Moreover, the 'German' units in the area were also full of 'volunteers' from many nations and in France there were 45 *Ost* (East) battalions, recruited among former Soviet prisoners of war, whose reliability was uncertain. In accordance with Rommel's plan to stop an invasion, most of the German divisions in the area were 'static' or 'coastal' formations without integral motor transport and reliant instead on horsed transport and marching for their mobility. Small arms ammunition was plentiful, but transport bottlenecks caused by Allied bombing and sabotage led to local shortages of artillery ammunition. The many foreign weapons in use only exacerbated the problem. *General der Infanterie* Günther Blumentritt, chief of staff at OB West from 6 June 1944, asserted that the coastal divisions were:

Rommel receiving his field marshal's baton from Hitler in October 1942. Field Marshal Walter Model said that he was, 'One of the greatest of German commanders... with a lightning power of decision, a soldier of the greatest bravery and of unequalled dash. Always in the front line, he inspired his men to new deeds of heroism by his example.' *(IWM FLM1429)*

> '... unaccustomed to mobile warfare in open terrain. Most of the officers and men had been wounded and were in limited assignment status. Their weapons were no match against a modern, well equipped enemy.'
>
> *Source*: David C. Isby, *Fighting The Invasion*.

These divisions were to defend *in situ* and certainly could not rely on the *Luftwaffe* (German Air Force) for support in the event of an invasion for there were only just over 100 serviceable fighters and fighter-bombers covering France, Belgium and Holland. Even these were short of fuel and experienced crews.

Hitler's supposedly impregnable 2,700-km 'Atlantic Wall' was an attempt to put another obstacle in the way of any Allied assault from the sea. However, these defences were inadequate as they had little depth and lacked sufficient numbers of integral counter-attacking troops. The problem was resources; with hundreds of kilometres of coast to defend and many competing commitments, the Germans had to prioritise. Because of its proximity to England, the Pas de Calais seemed the most likely area for an invasion, and therefore soaked up most of the

German Forces in the Orne Bridgehead Area
6 June 1944

21st Panzer Division

GenMaj Edgar Feuchtinger

22 Panzer Regiment	*Oberst von Oppeln-Bronikowski*
125 Panzergrenadier Regiment	*Major von Luck*
192 Panzergrenadier Regiment	*Oberstleutnant Rauch*
21 Panzer Reconnaissance Battalion	*Major Waldow*
155 Panzer Artillery Regiment	*Oberstleutnant Huhne*
200 Assault Gun Battalion	*Major Becker*
200 Tank Hunter Battalion	*Hauptmann von Lynker*
305 Army Anti-Aircraft Battalion	*Hauptmann Ohlendorff*
220 Panzer Pioneer Battalion	*Hauptmann Hoegl*
200 Panzer Signals Battalion	*Hauptmann Huhnlich*

711th Infantry Division

GenLt Josef Reichert

731 Grenadier Regiment	*Oberst von Limburg*
744 Grenadier Regiment	*Oberst Maier*
1711 Artillery Regiment	
711 Pioneer Battalion	

716th Infantry Division

GenLt Wilhelm Richter

726 Grenadier Regiment	*Oberst Korfes*
736 Grenadier Regiment	*Oberst Krug*
1716 Artillery Regiment	*Oberstleutnant Knupe*
716 Tank Hunter Detachment	*Hauptmann Kärgel*
716 Pioneer Battalion	*Major Salzenburg*

346th Infantry Division

GenLt Erich Diestel

857 Infantry Regiment	
858 Infantry Regiment	
346 Artillery Regiment	
346 Pioneer Battalion	

Each German division also included administrative, signals, medical, military police and other support units.

resources. It was only latterly that the defences in Normandy were bolstered and the areas around the Rivers Dives and Divette were flooded to prevent an airborne assault near Caen.

In 6th Airborne Division's projected area of operations there were two German infantry divisions. 716th, part of Seventh Army's LXXXIV Corps, held a 45-km stretch of coast from east of Asnelles-sur-Mer to the River Dives. 711th, part of Fifteenth Army's LXXXI Corps, was responsible for the area east of the Dives. Gale's division was therefore to attack on the boundary not only between two divisions, but also between two corps and

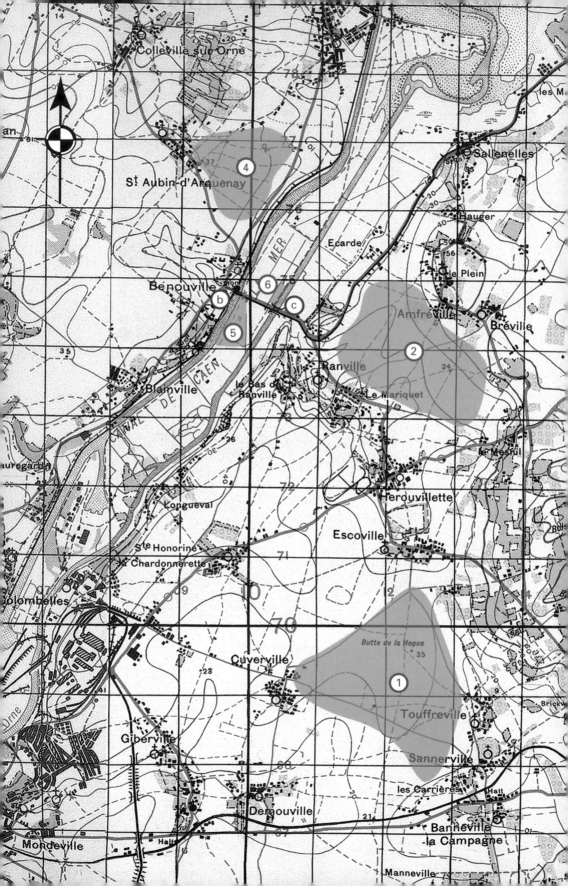

Franceville Plage
Merville

Bas Cabourg

Dives-su

Gonneville
sur-Merville

Les Boursiers

Périers-en-Auge

③

ⓗ
Varaville

Brucourt

la Rivière

Colleville

Petiville

Bavent

les Champs

Le Hoin

Robehomme

ⓖ St Clair

Bricqueville

Goustranville

Basseneville

ⓕ

le Mesnil
Halt

ⓔ Bures

St Richer

ⓓ

TROARN

Butte

THE AIRBORNE BATTLEFIELD

0   1   2
Kilometres

①	Drop Zone K	ⓑ	Bénouville (Pegasus) Bridge (to be captured)
②	Drop Zone N	ⓒ	River Orne bridge (to be captured)
③	Drop Zone V	ⓓ	Troarn bridge (to be destroyed)
④	Landing Zone W	ⓔ	Bures road bridge (to be destroyed)
⑤	Landing Zone X	ⓕ	Bures railway bridge (to be destroyed)
⑥	Landing Zone Y	ⓖ	Robehomme bridge (to be destroyed)
ⓐ	Merville Battery	ⓗ	Varaville bridge (to be destroyed)

Base maps: GSGS 4250 Troarn 7F2, Caen 7F1

Stirlings line up ready for the airborne operations on 5 June at RAF Keevil. Black and white stripes were painted around the wings and fuselages of all Allied Air Expeditionary Force aircraft in preparation for the invasion. *(IWM CH13298)*

two armies. For the Germans this was a potential weakness. *Generalleutnant* (GenLt) Richter, who had his headquarters at Caen, led 716th Infantry Division, which consisted mainly of 736th Grenadier Regiment, in the coastal defences, with small elements of 726th Grenadier Regiment in reserve to the west. The 736th Regiment, led by *Oberst* (Colonel) Ludwig Krug, straddled the Orne estuary but had its weight west of the river. The division's 1716th Artillery Regiment was based in Beuville to the west of the Caen Canal, with 1st Battery, 1716th Artillery, manning the Merville battery. 711th Infantry Division, led by *Generalleutnant* Josef Reichert, consisted of 731st Grenadier Regiment, stationed near the coast with its headquarters at Trouville, and 744th Grenadier Regiment, which was further west with headquarters at la Forge. It was supported by 1711th Artillery Regiment, comprising two battalions totalling 8 batteries, equipped with 16 Russian 76.2-mm guns and 16 French 155-mm howitzers. 346th Infantry Division at Le Havre was also a potential threat to the British airborne division, but as it was static it was considered unlikely to cause a serious threat quickly (although events were to prove otherwise). Moreover, the flooded area was a major obstacle to any counter-attacking formation and any move would be made all the more difficult if the paras destroyed the bridges over the Dives.

Behind these infantry divisions was the armour, but the way in which that armour was deployed had been the subject of much German discussion. In the end an untidy compromise was reached and 21st Panzer Division, commanded by *Generalmajor* (GenMaj) Edgar Feuchtinger, established its headquarters at St-Pierre-sur-Dives, some 25 km south-east of Caen. It was placed under the direct control of Army Group B. 12th SS Panzer Division *Hitlerjugend* and Panzer Lehr Division, however, were situated a considerable distance from the coast under the direct control of Hitler's headquarters in Germany. This command structure was hardly likely to allow for swift and flexible control.

21st Panzer Division was clearly a threat to 6th Airborne Division but was not yet fully operational, having been resurrected in Europe after being virtually wiped out in North Africa. It had been in the vicinity of Caen since the end of April, but was still re-equipping and retraining in the first week of June; so, as GenMaj Feuchtinger later commented, 'a panzer division of average mobility arose from wreckage and old iron'. It consisted of 22nd Panzer Regiment (two battalions); 125th

Maj-Gen Gale chatting with parachutists before they don their parachutes and emplane on 5 June. The aircraft in the background is an Armstrong Whitworth Albemarle. *(IWM H39068)*

A posed 1943 photograph of an airborne infantry platoon about to take off in a Horsa glider (looking aft). The cramped conditions and the flimsy wooden infrastructure can be clearly seen. Note the chest harnesses, the tiny porthole behind the first man on the left and the edge of the loading ramp door on the near right hand side. *(IWM CH10208)*

and 192nd Panzergrenadier Regiments (each comprising two battalions plus 9th (infantry gun) and 10th (rocket projector) Companies; 155th Panzer Artillery Regiment (three battalions of three batteries each, plus a 10th [rocket projector] Battery); 21st Panzer Reconnaissance Battalion (five companies); 200th Assault Gun Battalion (four batteries); 200th Anti-Tank Battalion (three batteries); 305th Flak Battalion (three batteries); and 220th Panzer Pioneer (Engineer) Battalion (three companies).

However, in the initial stages of the invasion it was *Major* Hans von Luck's 125th Panzergrenadier Regiment that was going to come into direct contact with the airborne division. Luck's HQ was at Vimont, 13 km south-east of Caen; his 1st Battalion was at Vierville and his 2nd Battalion, under *Hauptmann* (Captain) Kuron, had its headquarters at Colombelles, just 5 km north-east of Caen, with its companies based at Troarn, Banneville-la-Campagne, Ranville and Colombelles. However, the division was under strict orders not to launch any major counter-attack against enemy landings until cleared to do so by Army Group B.

The Allies had a good general idea of German strengths and weaknesses by June 1944 and Gale possessed detailed and reasonably accurate intelligence. His information revealed that there were excellent drop zones (DZs) and landing zones (LZs) close to British objectives, and that the ridge running south from the estuary of the Orne for 10 km to Troarn was crucial. The

north half of this ridge was covered with orchards and held the villages of Sallenelles, le Plain (marked on Allied maps in 1944 as Le Plein), Amfréville, and Bréville. To the south of Bréville was the dense Bois de Bavent, thick with trees and impossible to manoeuvre vehicles in without using its few roads. The ridge was an excellent position to defend and had to be denied to the Germans. To the west the country was more open, although still studded with orchards, large farm houses and thick hedges. It contained an ideal DZ/LZ and, to its south, the villages of Ranville, le Mariquet, Hérouvillette and Escoville. These stretched in a south-easterly line from the River Orne to the ridge. To the east of the ridge the ground fell away towards the Dives and the flooded lowlands. To the north was the coast, separated from the ridge by a thin strip of land. To the south was open ground, which would provide the Germans with many counter-attack opportunities even if 6th Airborne Division took all its other objectives.

A Horsa glider being loaded with a 6-pounder anti-tank gun shortly before the invasion. *(IWM H39084)*

Gale and his staff added this information to what they already knew about the German Army's operational methods and tactics – and particularly its counter-attacking potential – as they made their plan. They also had an inkling of the German command and control problems and were confident that airborne speed and surprise would hand Gale's men the initiative. The divisional plan settled, Gale called his brigade commanders to his planning HQ near Netheravon on 18 March and issued his orders for D-Day.

The plan was for a *coup de main* force (D Company, 2 OBLI, plus two platoons from B Company) to arrive by glider shortly after midnight on 6 June and capture intact the bridges over the Caen Canal and the Orne River between Bénouville and Ranville. This was to be followed shortly afterwards by the dropping of the two parachute brigades. 5th Para Brigade, with 4th Anti-Tank Battery, RA, (less one section) under command, was to secure and hold the area of Bénouville–Ranville–le Bas de Ranville. One of its three battalions, 7 Para, would be relieved that evening when 3rd Infantry Division advanced from the beaches. It would then move into reserve behind 12 and 13 Para, which had the task of fending off any German counter-attacks across the open ground on the southern flank. 5th Para Brigade was also responsible for clearing the LZ north of Ranville of obstructions to facilitate the safe arrival of both the 68 gliders containing the divisional headquarters at 0330 hours, and the 146 gliders of 6th Airlanding Brigade that were to arrive that evening. Meanwhile, 3rd Para Brigade (with one section of 4th Anti-Tank Battery under command) was to silence the Merville battery before heading for le Plain at the northern end of the Bavent Ridge. 1 Canadian Para was to destroy bridges over the Divette at Varaville and the Dives near Robehomme before holding the centre of the Bavent Ridge at le Mesnil. Finally, 8 Para was to destroy bridges near Bures and Troarn and deny the enemy use of the dense woods along the southern half of the ridge.

Gale considered that both the parachute brigades would be able to hold out against immediate counter-attack, but there needed to be greater depth to the bridgehead at Ranville. To achieve this, the 1st Special Service Brigade, commanded by Brigadier Lord Lovat and consisting of Nos. 3, 4 and 6 Commando and No. 45 (Royal Marine) Commando, was to land over the beaches, fight its way to the Bénouville bridge and come under Gale's command during the early afternoon. The brigade was then to move north-east, clear and hold the village of le Plain, and use this as a base to mop up resistance along the coast to the east through Sallenelles, Franceville-Plage and Cabourg. Only after the division had taken its objectives and mopped up all the resistance in the area could it be said to have secured the left flank and provided a springboard for further offensive action.

Deepening the bridgehead was the job of 6th Airlanding Brigade, which was to land in the second lift, on the evening of D-Day, along with the divisional armoured reconnaissance group. The landing force comprised 2 OBLI (less one company and two platoons) and 1 RUR. These troops were to take command of 4th Anti-Tank Battery from 5th Para Brigade on arrival and occupy and hold the bridgehead to the south-west of Ranville, in the area Longueval–Ste-Honorine–Escoville–le Bas de Ranville. 12th Battalion, Devonshire Regiment (12th Devons), less one company, and 3rd Anti-Tank Battery, RA, would join them after they had been landed over the beaches on D+1. The armoured reconnaissance group, known as Parkerforce because it was led by Colonel R.G. Parker, the deputy brigade commander, was to be prepared to operate against the open ground to the south of the bridgehead and to establish a firm base in the area of Cagny.

It consisted of 6th Airborne Armoured Reconnaissance Regiment, 211th Airlanding Light Battery, one troop of 3rd Anti-Tank Battery (to land by sea) and A Company of 12th Devons.

The plan was made as simple as it could be, but the nature of airborne warfare meant that there were certain complexities that just could not be ignored, not least the crucial relationship between the division and the RAF, upon whom the airborne forces relied in so many ways. Thus planning had to be conducted in close consultation with 38 Group, RAF, (flying Albemarles, Stirlings and Halifaxes for parachuting and glider towing) and 46 Group, RAF, (using Dakotas), which had to transport 6,000 parachutists, 20,000 containers, over 250 Horsa gliders and 30 Hamilcars. Although the division was to be carried in two lifts, which was hardly ideal, these lifts were at least to be on the same day. Moreover, bearing in mind lessons learned from previous operations, the DZs and LZs were close to the objectives and the link-up with the forces advancing from the beaches was intended to be swift.

The training intensified in April and then, having been told their missions (although not the precise location of their objectives), the component parts of the division split up for a time to refine their skills. Coming together again for important final exercises, 6th Airborne Division brought itself up to the pitch of excellence that Gale required. In his general instruction to officers on the conduct of the coming battle the general said that every commander at every level should know what was expected of him and emphasised the need for flexibility:

> 'You must remember that it is your plan, and it must be your duty to ensure that it is your plan which is being carried out. Your responsibility in this is not one that you can be permitted to shirk. Your natural tendency may be to fight shy of it. You cannot; for ultimately the edifice is yours, and its foundation and cornerstones must be laid by you... What you get by stealth and guts you must hold with skill and determination.'
>
> Source: Anon., By Air to Battle.

Towards the end of May the division, thoroughly prepared for the tasks that it was asked to carry out, was moved to the concentration areas it was to occupy until the troops were taken

Parachute Aircraft and Glider Tugs

Douglas Dakota

The Dakota (or C-47 in American service) was an excellent multi-purpose transport aircraft that was well suited for dropping parachutists and as a glider tug. No. 46 Group, RAF, was formed in January 1944 and all five squadrons were supplied with Dakotas, Marks I, III and IV being used for airborne operations. Each could carry 20 fully equipped parachutists who jumped from a door on the port side of the rear fuselage.

Armstrong Whitworth Albemarle

The Albemarle was designed as a medium bomber, although it was never used as such. It entered service in January 1943 and was soon being used by 38 Group, RAF, for towing airborne forces' gliders. The Mark V was employed for dropping parachutists and supplies through a large hole in the floor of the rear fuselage.

Short Stirling

The Stirling bomber was also converted for towing Horsa gliders and dropping parachutists in early 1944. It could carry 22 parachutists, who jumped through a hole in the underside of the rear fuselage, and drop 12 containers to support them (or 27 containers when there were no parachutists).

Handley Page Halifax

The Halifax bomber was converted for use in airborne operations from November 1942 for glider towing and was powerful enough to tug the massive Hamilcar. It was experimented with for dropping parachutists but could only carry between 10 and 16 men. The Halifax was, however, used for dropping heavy equipment such as jeeps and 6-pounder anti-tank guns.

to their airfields. It was here that the final details of the invasion, the full divisional plan, and the locations of the objectives were finally released. Although naturally nervous, the troops in the camps were confident and revealed a great desire to get into action. In the final days before the invasion Gale made a point of travelling round to all of the camps to address the assembled troops, and his brigade commanders did the same. Take-off was scheduled for the night of 4–5 June, but just before lunchtime on the 4th the invasion was postponed for 24 hours due to the bad weather. The men spent the afternoon of the 5th in compulsory rest and then in the late afternoon began to get ready again. Gale had prepared his division as carefully and keenly as possible for operations in Normandy. In 12 months he had fused its disparate elements together, cleverly anticipated its likely roles, trained his men thoroughly, and constructed a robust plan. Even so, Gale was an experienced enough officer to recognise the truth in the old military dictum that plans rarely survive first contact with the

HISTORY

The following text appears on the aircraft:
THE CHANNEL STOPP YOU, BUT NOT US
REMINDER COVENTRY PLYMOUTH BRISTOL LONDON
NOW ITS OUR TURN
YOU'VE HAD YOUR TIME YOU GERMAN S
WINHUNDS

Afternoon 5 June. Men of 6th Airlanding Brigade's Ox and Bucks Light Infantry enjoy a joke at RAF Harwell prior to take off. These men were destined to land on the west side of the Caen Canal at LZ W. *(IWM H39178)*

enemy and that battles always spring surprises. As Brigadier Hill of 3rd Para Brigade told his men on the eve of battle, 'Gentlemen, in spite of your excellent training and orders, do not be daunted if chaos reigns. It undoubtedly will.'

CHAPTER 3

INTO BATTLE, 6 JUNE

On the evening of 5 June 1944, the Germans in Normandy did not think an Allied invasion imminent, partly because of their belief that it was relatively late in the year to begin such an enterprise, but largely because of the stormy weather. The result was that Rommel was back in Germany that night and a number of Seventh Army Commanders were on their way to a wargame in Rennes. Thus, whilst a battalion of 125th Panzergrenadier Regiment of 21st Panzer Division was on an anti-airborne assault exercise, it was more common to find the defenders keeping to their dull routines, or enjoying the pleasures of Normandy. At 2215 hours, however, Fifteenth Army, including 711th Division, was put on high alert and manned its defences after messages from the BBC to the French Resistance were intercepted and correctly interpreted as a warning order for imminent invasion. This alert spread across the German Army in the West, but the only army not to get the message was Seventh Army.

In southern England, meanwhile, the men of 6th Airborne Division were being taken from their concentration areas to their airfields. The RAF's 38 Group flew from Brize Norton, Tarrant Rushton, Fairford, Keevil and Harwell and carried the *coup de main* force and 5th Para Brigade, whilst 46 Group carried 3rd Para Brigade and flew from Blakehill Farm, Down Ampney and Broadwell. The men tried to eat a last meal before emplaning, gave their equipment one final check, went through their own personal routines and just before 2300 hours the *coup de main* force for the bridges took off.

Pathfinders at their transit camp being briefed by Lieutenant Bob Midwood. The rapt attention in the faces of the men reveals a good deal about the tension that was inevitably in evidence in the final days before the invasion. *(IWM H39089)*

Six Horsa gliders, towed by six Halifax bombers, carried the platoons from the Ox and Bucks Light Infantry and some sappers, all commanded by Major John Howard. At around 0020 hours three gliders landed on LZ X adjacent to the Caen Canal and two on LZ Y adjacent to the River Orne – a third glider assigned to LZ Y mistakenly landed some 13 km away

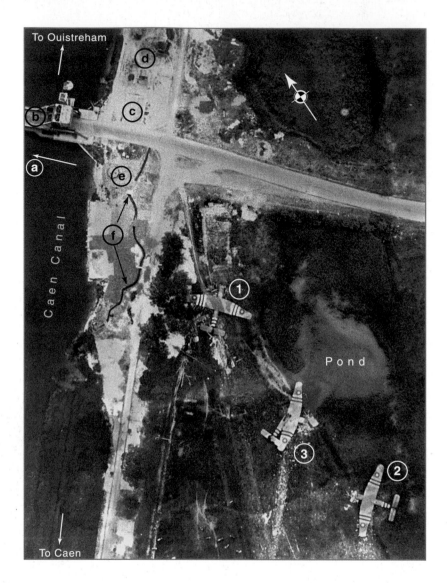

Aerial reconnaissance photographs taken on 6 June 1944. *(Museum of Army Flying)*

a. Café Gondrée
b. Bénouville (Pegasus) Bridge
c. Pill-box
d. Machine gun
e. Anti-tank gun
f. Slit trenches
g. Ranville (Horsa) Bridge
h. Machine guns

i. Pill-box
1. Glider No. 91 (Brotheridge & Howard)
2. Glider No. 92 (Wood)
3. Glider No. 93 (Smith)
4. Glider No. 96 (Fox)
5. (off photo) Glider No. 95 (Sweeney)

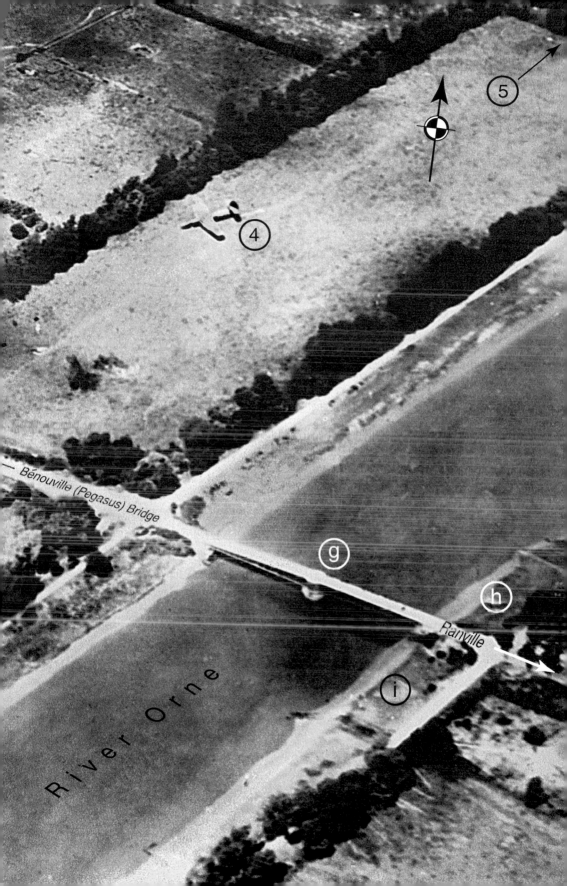

Bénouville (Pegasus) Bridge

River Orne

Ranville

④

⑤

g

h

i

next to a bridge over the River Dives. The gliders at the Caen Canal all landed extremely close to their objective and within minutes their occupants had overwhelmed the startled Germans at the bridge and established a defensive perimeter at the western end. The gliders at the River Orne did not land quite as close to their objective, but they took the bridge almost unopposed and then sent one platoon to reinforce the bridgehead at Bénouville. Having signalled his success, Howard and his men then waited for the arrival of 7 Para to relieve them, but before this reinforcement appeared they had to stop a half-hearted German armoured counter-attack. They knocked out the leading armoured vehicle with a PIAT (Projector Infantry Anti-Tank) on the western edge of the defensive perimeter, and the Germans withdrew and did not probe any further until dawn. (*For additional details on this operation see:* Tour A, *pages 107–127.*)

As the *coup de main* force tackled the bridges, 22 Independent Parachute Company (the pathfinders), dropped over DZs V, N and K from six Albemarles. There was a little scattering in this drop, but the problems caused by this were nothing when compared with the chaos that ensued when some of the

Pegasus Bridge from the west side of the Caen Canal on 12 June. Parts of two of Major Howard's three *coup de main* gliders can be seen on the right and extreme right. *(IWM B7032)*

Radar Homing Devices

Accurate insertion of airborne forces was always difficult during the Second World War, but in 1944 the Allies developed the Rebecca–Eureka guidance system. This required a pathfinder to set up a Eureka transmitter beacon on the ground prior to the main lift and send out and receive signals on one of five frequencies. A Rebecca was placed in each aircraft to receive the signal and respond to the Eureka and from that point the two would transmit to each other giving the pilots in the aircraft their bearing to, and distance from, the DZ or LZ from approximately 20 km away.

pathfinders failed to recognise that they had been dropped on DZ N rather than DZ K, and the consequences of all of the Eureka beacons having been broken on landing at DZ V. Following close behind these pathfinders were 21 Albemarles with the advance party for 5th Para Brigade and 16 Albemarles for 3rd Para Brigade. Brigadier Poett and his 5th Brigade team landed accurately on DZ N and linked up with Howard at Bénouville Bridge shortly after, but Brigadier Hill and 3rd Para Brigade had problems. Although 8 Para's advance party landed accurately on DZ K, on DZ V where the advance parties of

A posed photograph of four Pathfinder officers synchronising their watches before take-off at RAF Harwell – all survived the war. Left to right – Lieutenants Bobby de la Tour, Don Wells, John Vischer and Bob Midwood. This is one of the most famous and atmospheric images associated with the British Army and D-Day. *(IWM H39070)*

HISTORY

Airspeed Horsa glider

The Horsa glider became available after protracted trials during 1942. The aircraft was a monoplane with a tricycle undercarriage and a central skid. It was 20.4 m long with a 26.8 m wing span. The Horsa could carry a load of 3.15 tonnes and was made with a plywood skin over a wooden framework. The fuselage was circular in section, with wooden seats down each side, with each place having a safety harness. The glider carried two pilots and 29 passengers. There were two entrances, one on the left near the nose and the other on the right at the rear. The nose was hinged for loading and unloading and the entire tail was detachable to enable the rapid unloading of jeeps, anti-tank guns and other heavy materials. 12 Horsas were fitted with a pair of arrester parachutes for the *coup de main* attacks on the bridges and the Merville battery to help them to stop quickly.

brigade HQ, 9 Para and 1 Canadian Para were to have landed, six men jumped from one aircraft too early over the coast and were never seen again and another two aircraft had difficulty finding the drop zone and were then hit by flak.

When the main lift came in at 0050 hours, the difficulties encountered by the pathfinders were at least partly responsible for the scattering of the two parachute brigades. Consequently, 13 out of 21 sticks from 8 Para and two out of the six gliders which should have landed on DZ K ended up on DZ N instead. This severely delayed the battalion's assembly and movement to its objectives. At DZ V the broken Eurekas meant that pilots had to look for the two green lights that the pathfinders had placed there, but since the northern edge of the DZ was only 60 seconds' flying time from the coast, and visibility was severely hampered by the smoke and dust resulting from the bombing raid on the Merville battery just minutes before, finding the lights was extremely difficult. The result was that, for 9 Para and the Canadians, only 17 out of 71 aircraft dropped accurately over DZ V and both battalions were very badly scattered. The most successful drop was at DZ N, the destination for 110 Stirlings and Albemarles and 21 Dakotas. Aided by the distance of the DZ inland, the moon glinting off the waterways, the working Eurekas, the DZ lights and the pyrotechnics from the battle at Bénouville, 2,026 men and 702 containers were accurately dropped, the only difficulty being some flak and a westerly wind that drifted many to the eastern side of the DZ. It was, therefore, a mixed night for the two parachute brigades, but they were in enemy-held territory at last.

The *coup de main* party at the bridges was relieved by 7 Para at around 0300 hours. It had taken Lieutenant-Colonel (Lt-Col) Pine-Coffin's men a considerable time to find their rendezvous at le Home near the River Orne bridge. Nevertheless, at 0230 hours, although without mortars, heavy machine guns or radios, approximately 300 men moved off to their objective. Pine-Coffin was met at the canal bridge by Howard and Poett and his men quickly set up their defensive positions in Bénouville and le Port ready for the inevitable German counter-attacks. The enemy began to probe the extended bridgehead just after dawn with infantry, tanks and self-propelled guns, but 7 Para managed to hold its positions although taking some casualties. This began a tense time for the battalion. Pine-Coffin did not have radio contact with his companies, though he knew from runners and the sound of battle in late morning that the Germans were applying more pressure and forcing his men to concede ground. The situation looked decidedly healthier, however, when at 1300

Bénouville village looking north from the perimeter wall of the château. It was in this area that C Company, 7 Para, unleashed an ambush on some German armour which entered the village soon after dawn on 6 June. A Company fought in the vicinity for the rest of the day. *(Author)*

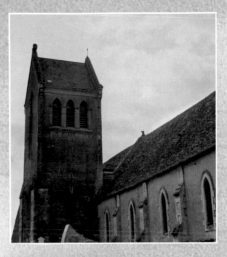

Then: The damage to the tower was caused by Cpl Killean (see p. 50). This photograph was taken on 10 June once le Port had been secured. The four soldiers are possibly from 2nd Royal Warwickshire Regiment. *(IWM B5429)*

Now: The restored church tower in le Port. *(Author)*

hours 1st Special Service Brigade reached Bénouville from the beaches. Lord Lovat's men wasted no time in crossing the waterways. As they pushed on to their objectives, the situation in Bénouville and le Port began to stabilise.

Fighting did not entirely die down, however. The 7 Para adjutant, Captain Richard Todd (later to become a famous actor), had made several attempts to put a German in the church tower at le Port out of action but had failed. Corporal Killean volunteered to have a go.

> **Captain Todd remembered what happened next.**
>
> 'He mouseholed through some cottages, going inside them and knocking holes through from one to the other so that he was able to get to the end cottage. He ran out and got his PIAT under a hedge and he let fly a bomb, and he hit a hole right where he wanted to in the church tower.'
>
> *Source:* Stephen Ambrose, *Pegasus Bridge*.

That evening troops from 3rd Division also reached the bridgehead and relieved 7 Para, who then marched back over the bridges to a reserve position on the western edge of DZ N.

After crossing the bridges over the Caen Canal and the River Orne, 4 Commando moved to Hameau Oger (often marked on 1944 maps as Hauger) and took up defensive positions, 6 Commando marched to le Plain and linked up with 9 Para, and 45 Commando pushed on to Merville village where it was tasked with denying the Germans the northern end of the Bavent Ridge. 3 Commando also crossed the bridges but was kept back by Gale as 12 Para was under pressure in le Bas de Ranville from German attacks emanating from Ste-Honorine. Having supplied one troop for a successful counter-attack that afternoon, the commandos waited until the danger had passed and then rejoined their brigade in le Plain that night.

Brigadier S.J.L. Hill, DSO, MC, of 3rd Para Brigade receiving a bar to his DSO from Montgomery. Hill had been a regular officer in the Royal Fusiliers before joining the Parachute Regiment. *(IWM BU4746)*

Part of the 6th Airlanding Brigade air armada just as it is about to cross the Normandy coast on the evening of 6 June, taken from a Halifax. Three Stirling tugs pulling Horsa gliders can be seen. *(IWM CL21)*

The 12 Para rendezvous was a quarry about 1.25 km north-east of the Orne Bridge. Amongst the first to arrive was the CO, Lt-Col A.P. 'Johnny' Johnson. It took the battalion about 45 minutes to begin to assemble. By 0230 over half their number had arrived and they moved off to le Bas de Ranville. The village was occupied without any difficulty and by 0400 hours 12 Para had begun digging in on a shallow arc from le Home, east of the Ranville Bridge, through the southern outskirts of le Bas de Ranville and out on the high ground to the south of the village towards Colombelles. At around dawn there were some German probes of the area from the south, which were repulsed, but in mid-morning the Germans put together a more formidable attack preceded by heavy mortaring. Approximately 100 infantry and two self-propelled guns moved forward against le Bas de Ranville. Although 12 Para held its position, the pressure on the battalion in the early afternoon made its situation (and that of 13 Para in Ranville – *see below*), look precarious. A counter-attack in the afternoon by A Company of 7 Para and a troop of 3 Commando from 1st Special Service Brigade, supported by the artillery of 3rd Infantry Division from across the river, forced the Germans back. Then, at around 2100 hours, there was a lull as

6th Airlanding Brigade began to land on LZ N and two fresh battalions began to swarm around the southern flank. (*For further details on this operation see: Tour C, pages 151–167.*)

British troops from 3rd Division look on as 6th Airlanding Brigade lands on the evening of 6 June. It is likely that containers hang underneath the parachutes which can be seen. (*IWM B5046*)

13 Para was also involved in defending against the German attacks that were launched against the southern flank. Two-thirds of the battalion had gathered at their rendezvous by 0150 hours, and they then headed off to Ranville. 591st Engineer Squadron and one of the 13 Para companies, however, stayed behind to clear the German anti-glider landing poles from DZ N and fill in the irrigation ditches across it in preparation for the glider landings that were soon to follow. By 0315 hours, just 15 minutes before the gliders began to land, the job was completed. The rest of 13 Para had, by 0400 hours, cleared Ranville of elements of 2nd Battalion, 125th Panzergrenadier Regiment, and begun digging in. The rest of the day was taken up with defending against various German attacks from the south (*see also above*). These included a probe by four self-propelled guns advancing from Hérouvillette, which was ended when 6-pounder guns knocked them out, and an infantry company attack from the same direction which was again rebuffed after some intense fighting. The arrival of 6th Airlanding Brigade that evening therefore provided a much welcomed influx of troops and a considerable boost to the morale of those units which had already come under fire.

8 Para was the most widely scattered of any battalion in the division as it was split between DZs K and N. Indeed, when Lt-Col Alistair Pearson reached the rendezvous on the eastern edge of DZ K (on the western outskirts of Touffréville) at 0120 hours he found only 30 men there. Two and a half hours later this number had increased to 11 officers and 145 other ranks, including 6 sappers, and equipment which amounted to a light machine gun, two PIATs, two jeeps and four radios, but the battalion was still well under strength. The plan was for Major Roseveare and his 3rd Parachute Squadron, RE, covered by the battalion, to blow the bridges at Troarn and Bures. Pearson's men would then move back and set up a firm base in the Bois de Bures and Bois de Bavent, in order to patrol vigorously and halt any German movement from the east and south-east. There were difficulties from the outset however. Roseveare, together with many of his squadron, landed on DZ N rather than DZ K and this caused disorientation that was not conducive to a speedy get-away.

The woods of the Bois de Bavent as experienced by 8 Para. Although there were occasional clearings, the woods were dense, dark and damp. This photograph was taken just off the D37b road which links Bréville with Troarn. *(Author)*

Even so, Roseveare linked up with some sappers and marched off to Troarn, picking up more men on the way. When the party reached the point where the road south from le Mesnil met the road from Escoville to Troarn, Roseveare sent the bulk of the sappers off on foot through the woods to the two bridges at Bures (a rail bridge to the north and a small road bridge to the east), whilst he and a small team packed into a medical jeep piled high with explosives and headed down into Troarn. After a short fire-fight, Roseveare's party managed to blow a 5-metre gap in the river bridge, and made their way back through the woods to le Mesnil to link up with brigade headquarters, which had landed on DZ V. The Bures party, meanwhile, was also successful in its mission and, having reached the two bridges at 0630 hours, destroyed them and then withdrew back to 8 Para in the Bois de Bures.

'Juckes Bridge' at Bures. Lieutenant Juckes was sent off by Major Roseveare to destroy the bridge here (in 1944 this was a short steel girder bridge) with a party of sappers in the early hours of 6 June whilst Roseveare made a dash for the bridge at Troarn. Juckes successfully completed this mission and he and his men then went on to the 8 Para battalion position in the Bois de Bures. *(Author)*

Whilst the bridges were being destroyed, Pearson's men struggled to reach their battalion rendezvous. Meanwhile his headquarters company tried unsuccessfully to contact Roseveare and the rest of the engineer squadron. Recognising the importance of destroying the bridges, and with no information as to whether they had been made impassable or not, Pearson sent a party to blow the bridges at Bures. However, he decided that he would wait until he had enough men before tackling Troarn, as locals had told him that panzergrenadiers with armoured half-tracks held the village.

At 0400 hours the battalion was still very weak, but it moved off north-east into the Bois de Bures and dug in at a cross-track just east of the main Troarn–le Mesnil road. En route, two PIAT

The Bois de Bavent area. *(Base map: Staff College 1947 tour map)*

detachments were dropped off and shortly afterwards successfully ambushed six fully-loaded German half-tracks.

During the morning the strength of the battalion rose and patrols were sent out to assess the situation in Troarn as Pearson had still not heard from Roseveare. In order to ensure that the bridge there was blown, a party was sent to destroy the bridge or widen the gap if the job had already been done. After a tough fight against elements of 21st Panzer Division's reconnaissance battalion, the party managed to increase the gap in the bridge to 20 metres before returning to the battalion.

By 1800 hours 8 Para was 17 officers and 300 men strong with two 3-inch mortars, a German 81-mm mortar, three Vickers machine guns, six PIATs and six radios. By the end of the day, in spite of its inauspicious start, the battalion had destroyed the bridges at Bures and Troarn, dominated the woods from a point just south of le Mesnil to the Troarn Road and was ready to fend off any German counter-attacks that came its way.

9 Para was tasked with protecting the northern end of the Bavent Ridge on 6 June, but the battalion's first objective was the Merville battery approximately 2 km west of DZ V. The four casemates of this battery were protected by a strong garrison and belts of barbed wire and minefields, and so the battalion was split into various parties to facilitate entry into the complex and to destroy the guns. A reconnaissance party was to examine the defences and report their findings to the CO; a taping party was to clear routes through the minefield; and a rendezvous party was to organise the battalion after it had dropped. The majority of the battalion was to assault the casemates after a glider-borne *coup de main* force had landed inside the battery and a breaching party had blown gaps in the barbed wire.

Unfortunately for the CO, Lt-Col Terence Otway, his plan was immediately undermined when his battalion was scattered over an area of 130 square kilometres. Thus, with just a tiny fraction of his specialist equipment and only 150 men, Otway moved off towards his objective, rethinking his assault as he went. By the time that the battalion arrived at the perimeter of the battery, the taping party had done their best to clear the minefield without their mine detectors and to mark the routes without tape. With the battalion briefed about the revised plan, at 0430 hours the breaching and assault parties watched as only two of the three expected *coup de main* gliders appeared overhead, and then

The main road through Troarn leading down to the bridge over the Dives. Although this was already successfully destroyed by Roseveare and his men, Pearson had received no word from the sappers and so sent out another party to deal with the objective. Lieutenant Brown's 9 Platoon from B Company provided the support for a team of sappers led by Lieutenant Juckes. Emerging from the road beside the church on the left of this picture, the party then fought their way down the hill against elements of 21st Panzer Division's reconnaissance battalion. A 20-metre gap was blown in the already ruined bridge before the men returned to the battalion for the loss of just two casualties. *(Author)*

missed their target under heavy anti-aircraft fire. Nevertheless, two gaps were blown in the wire, the attack was put in and after an immensely confusing fight lasting around 20 minutes, the four guns were disabled. (*For additional details about this operation see:* Tour B, *pages 127–151.*)

HISTORY

The Merville Battery

The battery commander was *Leutnant* (2nd Lt) Raimund Steiner, who spent much of his time at an observation post on the coast; his second-in-command was *Oberfeldwebel* (Sgt-Maj) Hans Buskotte. Casemate No. 1 was a Type 611 and consisted of the gun housing, access corridor and two ammunition stores (one for shells and one for cartridges), a shelter for 9 artillerymen, a gas extraction chamber and a machine-gun embrasure covering the rear. It was 15.5 m long and required over 1,330 cubic metres of concrete, and 65 tons of steel rods in its construction. It could house a 150-mm gun. It took two years to complete, and then the command bunker and other installations followed. The other casemates were Type 669s and used less material – 450 cubic metres of concrete and only 20 tons of steel.

Rendezvousing again just to the south of the battery, Otway found that he only had 80 men still standing. At 0600 hours they moved off for le Plain, the battalion's second objective. They reached the crossroads between le Plain and Hameau Oger at around 0900 hours and came under enemy fire. A counter-attack retrieved the situation and the battalion moved into some houses at the northern end of le Plain where it was again attacked. Reinforced by 20 or so new arrivals, Otway put in a counter-attack against a large house some 300 metres away, the centre of German resistance, but this failed. Too weak to seize the village, the battalion set up a defensive position at Château d'Amfréville and awaited the arrival of 1st Special Service Brigade.

Officers of 9 Para in February 1944 (before Otway became CO) taken in front of the Officers' Mess, Kiwi Barracks, Bulford Camp. Mentioned in the text: *Front row* – Capt The Hon. Paul Greenway (extreme left); Maj G.E. Smith (fourth from left); Maj T.B.H. Otway (fifth from left); Maj A.J.M. Parry (fourth from right); *Middle row* – Lt M.J. Dowling (fifth from left); *Back row* – Lt H.C. Pond (fourth from left) and Lt A.R. Jefferson (fourth from right). *(IWM HM64125)*

The 1st Canadian Parachute Battalion had a number of objectives on 6 June, but the most critical were the protection of DZ V for the main lift, the destruction of the bridge at Varaville and Robehomme, and the seizing of the road junction on the high ground at le Mesnil. By creating a firm base on the ridge the battalion was to prevent enemy observation of the Bénouville bridgehead, thwart any German counter-attacks from the east and protect 3rd Para Brigade headquarters, which was also to be established in the area. The Canadians' ability to attain these objectives was, however, dealt a body blow by the scattering at DZ V that morning. Nevertheless, after a long fight with the garrison at a headquarters in Varaville, the Germans were kept at bay around DZ V, the two bridges were destroyed and gradually

Taken from Troarn looking north-east, this photograph shows the area beside the Dives which was flooded by the Germans. It was in areas like this that the scattered troops destined for DZ V ended up – many were drowned. *(Author)*

the battalion gathered at the le Mesnil crossroads. Brigadier Hill arrived at his HQ at 1400 hours having swum the Dives, been wounded by Allied bombs, visited 9 Para, seen Gale at divisional headquarters and been operated on by the division's medics.

The divisional headquarters visited by Hill landed at 0335 hours on DZ N with other elements, such as 225 Parachute Field Ambulance (the unit which operated on Hill later). Gale landed in one of the 20 divisional headquarters gliders that took off from England. Other gliders brought in 4th Anti-Tank Battery which, with 3rd Anti-Tank Battery, provided crucial firepower for the lightly armed airborne forces. By the evening the division was also be able to call on the 75-mm howitzers of 211th Airlanding Light Battery, RA, which arrived with 6th Airlanding Brigade; as well as the artillery of 3rd Infantry Division and I Corps, which had landed over the beaches. In addition to these guns, two cruisers, HMS *Arethusa* and HMS *Mauritius*, and two destroyers were to provide fire support from off the coast if required via Forward Observers Bombardment (FOBs – army officers trained in naval gunnery procedures).

Divisional headquarters, accompanied by Brigadier Kindersley who arrived early in order to assess the situation on the ground before his 6th Airlanding Brigade landed, established itself at the Château de Heaume in Ranville at around dawn and soon found itself under German artillery fire. At 0700 hours, radio silence was broken and the division endeavoured to contact the two parachute brigades. Poett, whose headquarters was in a farm between the château and the bridges, had already been to see Gale and appraise him of the situation, but there was difficulty contacting 3rd Para Brigade which, unknown to Gale, was without its brigadier, radio operator and sets owing to the scattering. Nevertheless, as noted, Hill turned up in Ranville later that morning, and by the evening division had established full contact with his headquarters. With his two parachute brigades having achieved considerable success, the first counter-attacks repelled, the arrival of 6th Airlanding Brigade awaited and the link with 1st Special Service Brigade completed, Gale felt as satisfied as could be expected on such a challenging day.

THE GERMANS AND THE AIRBORNE LANDINGS

The German reaction to the airborne landings was not helped by the inherent weaknesses in their command and control system. In addition the unintentional scattering of the Allied paratroops caused great confusion as it misled the Germans as to the area and extent of the landings. Nevertheless, as soon as the landings began, the divisions in the area were put on high alert. *Major* Hans von Luck, commander of 125th Panzergrenadier Regiment of 21st Panzer Division, had also made it clear to his subordinate commanders that, if subjected to an airborne attack, they were to use their initiative locally and counter-attack as swiftly as they could. Thus, as soon as reports came in from his 2nd Battalion that it had engaged British paratroopers (largely men from 8 Para), the battalion immediately struck out towards Troarn,

OUISTREHAM

Water Tr.

SALTINGS

Mud

Mud

Mud

Sa

W

301

20

Quarries

River Orne

Quarries

Ch^au de

le
Port

Bénouville

Sta

Pont Tournant

le Longueville

X

N

Tr.

le Hom

Pegasus Bridge and the
nearby Drop and
Landing Zones.
(Base map: Staff College
1947 tour map)

le Bas de
Ranville

Ranville

le Mariquet

29

30
(R.496)

Touffréville, Escoville and Sannerville. Meanwhile, to the west of the Orne, two sections of 1st Tank Hunter Company (*1. Panzerjäger Kompanie*) set off from Biéville towards the Bénouville Bridge where they were stopped by a well-aimed PIAT round at 0130 hours (*see pages 122–124*). The rest of this unit, together with other troops from 716th Infantry Division, attacked 7 Para later that morning along with men from 192nd Panzergrenadier Regiment of 21st Panzer Division.

Château de Bénouville , looking south from the towpath beside the Caen Canal. Corporal Wally Parr fired on this building with the captured anti-tank gun at the east end of Pegasus Bridge as he thought it was an enemy observation post. In fact the building was being used as a maternity hospital whose director, Madame Vion, was the leader of the Resistance in Bénouville. *(Author)*

Meanwhile, Feuchtinger tried desperately to get authorisation from Army Group B to launch a full-scale counter-attack – but was refused. After the bombardment of the beaches began that morning Feuchtinger again asked for permission to unleash his armour. Again he was refused, although he was allowed to use his panzergrenadiers to attack Ranville. Consequently 125th Panzergrenadier Regiment launched a weak attack against the British southern flank soon after dawn, and a stronger push was made in mid-morning. During the day the attacks were gradually reinforced by 21st Panzer Division's reconnaissance battalion; 200th Assault Gun Battalion (five companies each with six 105-mm self-propelled guns, four 75-mm guns, a multiple mortar platoon and 20-mm AA guns); a battalion of tanks from 22nd

Panzer Regiment; and a platoon of 88-mm anti-tank guns. With orders to 'crush 6th Airborne's bridgehead, recapture the two Orne bridges at Bénouville and establish contact with the coastal units', these forces put 12 and 13 Para under great pressure. Although the airborne troops retrieved the situation during the afternoon, these German forces would continually harass, shell and counter-attack the southern flank for the next week.

By 0745 hours Army Group B was much less certain that the invasion was the feint that it had originally thought and released 21st Panzer Division to the control of LXXXIV Corps. This news took two hours to reach Feuchtinger. However, on his own initiative he had already primed 120 tanks and 3,000 infantry to move against Ranville, which was at that time defended by fewer than 1,000 lightly armed airborne soldiers with just a handful of anti-tank guns. At first General Marcks was minded to allow the division to make its counter-attack to the east of the Orne, but at 1030 hours Feuchtinger was told to switch his main effort to Caen and up the west of the canal to the coast. As a result Gale was spared. Feuchtinger was not pleased by the fragmentation of his division but later said that, 'the combat tasks which cropped up on both sides of the Orne all had a fateful influence on the course of the combat on 6 June 1944.'

Airborne soldiers escorting German prisoners towards Ranville during the afternoon of 6 June. These men had fought briefly in a nearby château before being overwhelmed. One of the men has had a field dressing applied to a wound on his left hand. *(IWM B5060)*

After the German counter-attacks on Ranville were repulsed, at just before 2100 hours 6th Airlanding Brigade and the 6th Airborne Division Armoured Reconnaissance Regiment began to land. 248 gliders safely reached LZs W and N, out of the 258 that left England, containing 1 RUR, the Armoured Reconnaissance Group, the balance of 2 OBLI, brigade headquarters, and some other divisional troops. Kindersley was waiting for them and immediately set off to establish his headquarters in an orchard in le Bas de Ranville. With the task of expanding the divisional perimeter to the south, Lt-Col Jack Carson's 1 RUR moved off to prepare for their attack on Longueval and Ste-Honorine the next morning, although C Company took the opportunity that night to establish themselves on the 'Ring Contour' (a prominent area of high ground about 1 km south of le Bas de Ranville). Lt-Col Michael Roberts' 2 OBLI moved through Ranville in order to take Escoville. The armoured reconnaissance group was to push south and watch for the approach of German tanks. The Devons and the light battery successfully reached their rendezvous with Colonel Parker near le Mariquet. However, soon after landing, 11 of the light Tetrarch tanks were entangled in the rigging lines of parachutes and were immobilised and two more were made unserviceable when two Hamilcar gliders collided on landing. Even so, the arrival of 6th Airlanding Brigade was a success. With the majority of Kindersley's men having arrived in the divisional area, Gale had attained the offensive capability that he required to safeguard his bridgehead. He wasted no time in using it.

General Aircraft Hamilcar glider

The Hamilcar was a massive wooden glider some 33.5 m long, with a wing span of 20.7 m and could carry a load of 7.9 tonnes. It was designed to carry armoured vehicles, guns and other heavy equipment and had to be tugged by powerful Halifax bombers. The Hamilcar had a hinged nose and was designed to use the weight of the cargo to tip the aircraft forward on landing so that there was no need for a ramp when unloading. The crews of the cargo vehicles remained in them throughout the trip and when nearing the ground would start their engines for a fast get-away.

By the end of 6 June the division was well set. The first lift had been far from perfect in all areas, but training, flexibility and good leadership had helped the airborne troops to move deftly towards the attainment of their first day objectives. Although the division still had much to achieve before the left flank could be said to be secure, it had made an extremely good start. The task on 7 June was to expand the divisional area, both in the north and the south, and meet and defeat any German counter-attacks that came their way.

An RAF reconnaissance photograph of DZ N showing discarded parachutes and Horsa gliders. Many of the gliders' tails have been detached for rapid unloading. A Hamilcar glider (a slightly different shape from the Horsa when seen from above) is near the bottom right hand corner of the photo. *(IWM CL59)*

CHAPTER 4

CONSOLIDATION, 7–9 JUNE

On 7 June, 6th Airborne Division, having successfully defended its positions during the night, continued with its defensive work and also sought to increase its bridgehead after the arrival of 6th Airlanding Brigade. The Germans, of course, having had time to recover from the initial surprise of the invasion, endeavoured to

The southern flank. *(Base map: Staff College 1947 tour map)*

N

le Ho

le Bas de
Ranville

Ranville

le Mariquet

30
(R.496)

Herouvil

Fe de Lieu
Haras

Longueval

Ste. Honorine
la Chardonerette

23

Butte de la Ho

30

Cuverville

K

30

do all that they possibly could to hinder these operations. German efforts in the south were focused on 125th Panzergrenadier Regiment, which sought both to stop the paras from encroaching any further in that direction and also wished to attack the British bridgehead itself. The trouble for the Germans in this area was that their flank and rear were constantly threatened by British troops from the areas of Troarn, Touffréville and Sannerville, and so they also had to develop operations to contain the airborne troops in these areas as well, which diluted their offensive capability.

In the early hours of 7 June 1st Canadian Para was attacked by some forward elements of 346th Infantry Division's 857th and 858th Grenadier Regiments, supported by self-propelled guns and a number of Panzer IVs. One tank managed to penetrate to within 100 metres of the crucial le Mesnil crossroads before withdrawing and the Canadians suffered some casualties. Clearly the Germans understood the importance of this road junction and, although this probing attack was repulsed, it served as a salutary reminder that the Germans would not give up the ground without a fight. 1st Special Service Brigade, meanwhile, dug in at the northern end of the Bavent Ridge: 6 Commando was in le Plain facing Bréville; 3 Commando in Amfréville; 4 Commando in Hameau Oger; and 45 (RM) Commando in

The Rue de 4 Commando in Hameau Oger. Throughout Normandy the destruction that the battles wrought has long since been cleared away leaving only memorials and road names to remind inhabitants and visitors alike of what once happened there. *(Author)*

Merville. Establishing a strong position in this area was critical, indeed more important than clearing the coastal area on D+1, and so time was spent consolidating here. The day started quietly, but later 6 Commando was harassed by shelling from Bréville. The high ground on the ridge here overlooked much of the critical area down towards and including the bridges over the Orne and the Caen Canal. Consequently, a counter-attack was launched by the commandos to clear that village but, finding the enemy there in strength, the commandos withdrew with prisoners, information and some weaponry, but also with the knowledge that this important position remained in German hands.

While this was happening 45 Commando was pulled back towards the rest of the brigade from Merville, where it had become isolated. During the afternoon, however, the marines were ordered to take Franceville, thereby denying the Germans the ability to outflank the northern British positions on the ridge whilst also safeguarding the troops who continued to land on Sword Beach. Two troops of 3 Commando therefore attacked the recently reoccupied Merville battery in order to prevent the Germans there from interfering with the attack. Although they failed to retake it, they did enough to divert the attention of the battery garrison and enable 45 Commando to reach Merville village. Following a bombardment of Franceville and the northern coastal fortifications by the 15-inch guns of HMS *Warspite*, at 1705 hours 45 Commando advanced and a lodgement was made in the town. The strength of the Germans in the area, however, forced the commandos gradually to relinquish their newly-won ground and eventually they withdrew.

Meanwhile, with the arrival of 1st Special Service Brigade in the Amfréville–le Plain area, 9 Para was free to link up with the rest of its brigade to the south of Bréville. As a result, the battalion moved to a new position near the Château St-Côme at the Bois du Mont, south of Bréville, late on 7 June. Otway only had about 90 men at this time, but on reaching their destination these men dug in astride the Bréville–le Mesnil road and prepared for patrolling and defensive operations.

In the early morning of 7 June 6th Airlanding Brigade prepared to undertake attacks to expand the southern portion of the bridgehead. 2 OBLI shared Ranville with 13 Para and from here moved off to take Escoville under the covering fire of the

7 June – an unidentified corner of an LZ revealing several Horsa gliders. Although earlier versions of the Horsa landed on a wooden skid, by 1944 the gliders landed on wheels as this lengthened the landing run and allowed greater control by the pilot so that more gliders could be parked in a smaller space. Nevertheless, as can be seen in this photograph, the skid was retained in order to provide some security if the undercarriage collapsed on impact with the ground. (IWM B5202)

anti-tank battery guns concealed in the woods along the southern flank. 1 RUR, meanwhile, with one company on the Ring Contour, made ready to attack the village of Longueval from which both bridges were under direct observation. At 0900 hours, A and B Companies moved off along the east bank of the Orne towards their objective covered by their colleagues on the high ground. Carson found Longueval unoccupied and ordered his men to dig in, but his C Company on the Ring Contour was in full view of the Germans in Ste-Honorine and was heavily mortared by 125th Panzergrenadier Regiment and bombarded by 200th Assault Gun Battery. Having brought up his reserve company, Carson decided to launch a two-company attack on Ste-Honorine from Longueval, but communication difficulties, a lack of ammunition and vigorous German defence led to its failure and the battalion was forced back on Longueval. The

Germans hit back almost immediately with a counter-attack onto the crest of the Ring Contour, but this was repelled and three German tanks were knocked out before they withdrew back into Ste-Honorine.

The continued German occupation of Ste-Honorine meant that there was still considerable danger to the bridgehead from that direction and also that Ranville and le Bas de Ranville remained under German mortar and shell fire, which threatened the divisional headquarters and those of two of Gale's brigades. Carson's men, meanwhile, set up a defensive perimeter in Longueval and waited. Overlooked on three sides and under constant fire from the Germans, they largely remained in this position until relieved on 14 June.

7 June, DZ N. Men of 1st Special Service Brigade look on as three German prisoners are taken away by jeep. The British officer, a captain, is identifiable by his binoculars and the pips on his shoulder. *(IWM B5203)*

The Ox and Bucks' attack on Escoville also failed to go according to plan. Although successfully occupying Hérouvillette, which was undefended, the battalion, commanded by Major Darell-Brown in the absence of Lt-Col Roberts (who had been injured on landing), found problems on entering Escoville when it ran into tanks and self-propelled guns. After some close-quarter fighting with the German infantry, the battalion – which did not have any fire support – withdrew. Casualties were heavy and

Major Howard's company (now with the main body of the battalion) lost half its strength in the attack. The outcome was that Gale decided that Escoville was not a critical objective and ordered that the southern outskirts of Hérouvillette were to be the limit of the flank. Thus, 6th Airlanding Brigade formed, in the words of the GOC, the 'horns on either flank of the Ranville position'. It was not a triumphant day for Kindersley's men, but they were buoyed by 12th Devons' arrival in le Bas de Ranville that evening. This battalion immediately relieved 12 Para, allowing Johnson's men to go into divisional reserve north of the Orne bridge at a quarry.

A Bren gun carrier crosses the Caen Canal at Bénouville from the east on 8 June. The traffic that came across this bridge during the first days of the invasion was considerable and provided the main supply line for 6th Airborne Division as it fought to establish control on the left flank. (IWM B5234)

By 7 June Gale had planned for the armoured reconnaissance group to be active on the southern flank with a firm base in the area of Cagny, to provide the division with information about German troop movements in this sector. However, from information received about the enemy from other sources, Gale judged that the situation did not justify sending this vulnerable force on its original mission and so disbanded the group,

The 1st Canadian Parachute Battalion Memorial at le Mesnil crossroads. This vital thoroughfare was attacked incessantly by the Germans during the first week of the battle as it was such an important position for movement around the Bavent Ridge and for observation from the high ground. The Canadians lost heavy casualties in the ferocious fighting here, but they held the position. *(Author)*

redeploying its parts where he determined they would be most valuable. The Armoured Reconnaissance Regiment, for example, was sent to create a firm base in the area held by 8 Para in the Bois de Bavent and from here it struck out in various directions.

In spite of certain difficulties encountered in extending the southern portion of the bridgehead, the situation by the end of 7 June continued to be satisfactory for Maj-Gen Gale. The bridges were still secure over the Caen Canal and the River Orne, the southern flank was not in any immediate danger, the enemy were being held on the eastern flank and the vast majority of the Bavent Ridge was in British hands. As for the gaps in the British

HISTORY

The bridge over the River Orne taken from the east side. The trees that can be seen beyond the truck on the bridge are in the vicinity of LZ Y (IWM B5230)

line, Bréville was denied to the Germans, for the time being, by patrolling, and the hole between 9 Para at St-Côme and 2 OBLI in Hérouvillette to the south was covered by mines laid by 13 Para. The left flank of the Allied invasion was still not secure but it was solid and Gale was obsessed with keeping it that way.

8 June did not see any let up in the German attempt to dislodge the airborne division or the special service brigade from their positions. At first light the Canadians at le Mesnil were again attacked by troops from 346th Infantry Division, having also come under heavy shell and mortar fire the previous night. The positions held by Lt-Col Bradbrooke's tired men were infiltrated that morning and at one point a tank separated his B and C Companies before it was hit twice by a PIAT and withdrew. A counter-attack by the Canadians restored the situation, but they had suffered heavy casualties.

This was a typical battle sequence in the Orne Bridgehead: a German counter-attack, close-quarter fighting, stoic defence, a German withdrawal followed by an Allied counter-attack; all costing both sides heavy casualties. With such intense fighting it was clear that resources were a critical factor in this battle. Gale's lines of communication were working well, with his brigades being successfully supplied by air and from the beaches, and he took comfort from the thought that 51st (Highland) Division was waiting in the wings to relieve his men at the appropriate time.

The Germans, however, found it difficult to supply their forward units properly owing to the massive impact of Allied air superiority. Nevertheless, they did what they could to reinforce the divisions that had come directly under the Allied cosh and, as expected, their 346th Infantry Division moved west from Le Havre in ever increasing numbers. Thus, at 0830 hours on 8 June, 1st Special Service Brigade found itself fighting against 857th Grenadier Regiment, supported by units from 711th Infantry Division's 744th Grenadier Regiment. These German attacks were poorly co-ordinated and not supported by artillery, but they lasted all day and pushed 4 Commando hard at Hameau Oger before being rebuffed with the help of 3 Commando.

There was also heavy fighting around Merville where 45 Commando was heavily attacked at 0930 hours by infantry supported by artillery, mortars and self-propelled guns. Although

Graves in Amfréville of men from 3 Commando, photographed on 15 June. (IWM B5603)

the German advance was stopped, 45 Commando became very short of ammunition and during the evening withdrew back into the brigade position at Amfréville. Although thus ultimately seemingly futile, 45 Commando's action at Merville did much to safeguard the northern end of the ridge, by diluting the German attacks in the area and inflicting heavy casualties at a time when its own brigade was at full stretch.

9 Para, meanwhile, patrolled out of the defensive position at St-Côme and the Bois du Mont and found the nearby château empty, although the battalion lacked the manpower to occupy it themselves. During the morning the Germans probed Otway's positions, but it was not until the afternoon that heavier attacks began. In common with many German moves around this time,

The view ESE from the Bavent ridge at St-Côme, the area of much fighting by 9 Para. The brown field in the middle distance formed part of DZ N with the village of Ranville discernible on the right hand side. Longueval cannot be seen, but is beyond the red and white striped chimney near the centre of the photograph. The Ring Contour is to the right of the water tower on the left edge and the city of Caen is in the far distance. *(Author)*

they were uncoordinated and unsupported by the sort of firepower that could have seriously undermined the physical defences of the British troops and their morale. As a consequence, 9 Para rebuffed the advances and held its position. Nevertheless, the Germans did find a gap between 9 Para and the commandos at Amfréville and reoccupied Bréville. This made movement along the Bréville–le Mesnil road extremely hazardous, which had the unfortunate result of isolating 9 Para even more.

8 Para was under less immediate pressure and spent its time constantly patrolling the woods at the southern end of the ridge with the Armoured Reconnaissance Regiment and pushing out to the south towards the Dives and the villages in the area. The terrain was difficult and conditions were uncomfortable because of the darkness of the woods and the mosquitoes, but a routine was established and the area was secure.

For the rest of the division the day was a quiet one with small-scale German attacks being dealt with and no ground being given. During the night of 7/8 June, however, 12th Devons in le Bas de Ranville were bombed by an enemy aircraft which killed three B Company men and wounded a further 17. In common with the rest of the division the men of the battalion responded to increasing mortar and artillery attack by ensuring that their slit trenches were even deeper and that they were adequately roofed for protection against mortar rounds bursting in the trees overhead. Their time was well spent for, on 8 June, the Germans poured fire relentlessly onto British positions on the southern flank, but this was disruptive rather than overtly dangerous to well-dug-in troops.

A typical narrow lane in the Bois de Bavent. Apart from along such thoroughfares, it was almost impossible for the Germans to move vehicles through the dense woods. As a result many of the actions involving 1st Canadian Para and 8 Para took place near roads and vital junctions. *(Author)*

The day was certainly not a happy one for the Ulster Rifles in Longueval, however. The battalion suffered five dead and a further nine wounded when 3rd Division guns inexplicably opened up on their positions that afternoon. Later a German patrol reached Carson's headquarters before being expelled and then armour targeted the HQ from the high ground to the north-east. After Carson's men radioed brigade headquarters for some help, two self-propelled 75-mm anti-tank guns arrived, one carrying Brigadier Kindersley himself, and after an exchange of fire during which neither the German tanks nor the British guns were hit, the enemy armour withdrew back to Ste-Honorine.

By the end of the day Gale had much to reflect on. 8 June had seen 1st Special Service Brigade come under increasing pressure from 346th Infantry Division, but the brigade had managed to stabilise the situation and by evening had even managed to strengthen its position. The crucial Bavent Ridge was also securely held by the division, but the German occupation of Bréville was a problem that would have to be solved sooner or later. The Germans in Ste-Honorine also continued to make nuisances of themselves without providing any real threat to the southern flank. The situation east of the Orne continued, therefore, to be stable. As 6th Airborne Division hung on tenaciously to its positions, the German forces found themselves being ground down and increasingly dislocated as the Allies pushed forward relentlessly across Normandy.

On 9 June the three German divisions ranged against Gale – the 711th in the extreme north, the 346th from Bréville to the south of le Mesnil, and the 21st Panzer Division further to the south – continued to apply pressure to the bridgehead. The 346th Division again attacked 1st Special Service Brigade, particularly in the area of Bréville and Sallenelles, but although the Germans achieved some infiltration, the attacks were more workmanlike than skilful and failed. 9 Para, however, found the Germans probing its positions at dawn but defended resolutely and forced the enemy to withdraw back to the relative safety of the woods near the château. Subsequent German attempts to overwhelm the battalion during the day failed, as did attempts to dislodge the nearby airborne troops at le Mesnil. Here 1 Canadian Para and

The driveway of the Château St-Côme around which there was so much fighting. There were many German probes from the left side of this photograph towards the driveway and the 9 Para defensive positions in the vicinity. *(Author)*

Taken from the le Mesnil–Bréville Road, the bungalow at the Bois du Mont can just be seen through the trees. It was here that 9 Para's battalion HQ and the reserve company were situated. In the clearing to the left of the building the battalion buried its dead (later reburied in the Ranville War Cemetery). *(Author)*

the 3rd Para Brigade HQ were threatened by a concerted German advance and so Otway rounded up 30 of his men and sent them south where they successfully helped to retrieve the situation.

By this stage 9 Para was 200 men strong, still too few to hope to occupy the château building, and so could only continue to patrol the area to try to dissuade the Germans from settling there. Otway established his HQ in a bungalow south of the Bréville road almost opposite the gates of the Château St-Côme. From here he played a game of cat and mouse with the enemy, judging that, since they had not overwhelmed 9 Para by this stage or managed to occupied the château, they must have their own weaknesses – a conclusion which gave hope to the defenders.

Thus, with 8 Para continuing to hold its position at the southern end of the ridge and 7 Para at the bridges, it was 6th Airlanding Brigade which was most active offensively on 9 June as it sought to expand the bridgehead. The artillery shelled Ste-Honorine during the night of 8/9 June and 1 RUR patrols and a radio message the next morning from division reported that the Germans were leaving the village. Acting quickly, Gale ordered Kindersley to move 12 Para from its reserve position to defend Longueval whilst 1 RUR attacked Ste-Honorine. However, reconnaissance groups sent out in preparation for the advance

Lt-Col R.G. Pine-Coffin, DSO, MC, commander of 7 Para (*centre*) with his RSM (*right*) and one of his men. *(IWM H42049)*

subsequently reported that the village was full of Germans and observers on the Ring Contour confirmed this. This information, and the news that no artillery support was available for the push, led Kindersley to cancel the attack. Shortly after, with two battalions packed into Longueval, the Germans shelled and mortared the village, causing many casualties. The situation was only retrieved after Kindersley jumped into a jeep and ordered the angry 12 Para survivors immediately back into reserve and 1 RUR to take over its old positions in the village.

The 2nd Ox and Bucks, meanwhile, still had their eyes on Escoville, but although a patrol was tentatively sent forward to assess the strength of the German positions there, it came up against strong opposition and had to withdraw. During this time heavy German fire came down on the le Bas de Ranville–Hérouvillette area and HQ 6th Airlanding Brigade was hit hard, as was the Ring Contour. This situation was not helped by a lack of close air support owing to bad

Brigadier J.H.N. Poett, commander of 5th Para Brigade. *(IWM H40778)*

weather. This restricted what the RAF could do but did not stop the *Luftwaffe* from attaining some unaccustomed freedom – enemy aircraft bombed and strafed British positions all day.

A tough day for 6th Airlanding Brigade was topped off that evening by heavy concentrations of mortar and rocket fire which were followed by smoke and an infantry assault by three companies of 125th Panzer-grenadier Regiment supported by tanks, which struck out to the left of the Devons' line at le Bas de Ranville. Silhouetted by their own smoke, however, the attackers provided good targets for the Devons, who hit them hard at 300 metres' range from the edge of the woods, and for the guns of 3rd Division and the anti-tank batteries. Encouraged by Brigadier Kindersley and their own Lt-Col Dick Stevens, the defenders inflicted heavy casualties on the Germans, who became fragmented and then lost all of their cohesion. An attack against Hérouvillette with tanks and self-propelled guns was also driven back by the Ox and Bucks, 13 Para and the anti-tank batteries, which knocked out two Panzer IVs and two self-propelled guns.

The battle in the south on 9 June was intense, bloody and exhausting, but the successful defence against the German onslaught had important consequences for British morale in what Gale called 'a very nervy kind of war'. The Germans had tried to batter the British in both the north and the south but failed to make a breakthrough because they failed to concentrate their resources with massed artillery fire in support. The British had been subjected to severe mortar, shell and self-propelled gun fire, but nothing as devastating as the concentrated fire of massed guns could have been. Showing themselves to be tactically rather naïve, therefore, the Germans found it difficult to oust the British from their strongholds at the crucial junctions, on the high ground and in their well hidden positions with uninterrupted fields of fire in the south. The British defences were tight but the Germans had not lost all hope, believing that the tired and lightly armed British might yet crack, and so the battle continued.

CHAPTER 5

PUSHING FORWARD, 10–12 JUNE

By 10 June the Bréville gap was becoming an area that the Germans were endeavouring to exploit. That morning they attacked from the village with approximately two battalions of infantry from 857th Grenadier Regiment of 346th Division, supported by artillery and armour, against 9 Para and 1st Special

A Bren gun carrier which had landed over Sword Beach passes a DZ N glider on the road from Ranville to Amfréville on 10 June. (IWM B5343)

Service Brigade in le Plain and Hameau Oger. Another prong of the attack struck out across DZ N, towards the crucial bridges and 13 Para on the southern edge of the DZ, and 7 Para on the western edge. As the Germans advanced in this area they proved easy pickings for the well-positioned British troops, particularly as they pushed forward here without any artillery or mortar support. This attack failed to make any important progress and by 1030 hours 6 Commando had rebuffed the attack at le Plain, which the Germans had tried to enter from the south. However, 4 Commando in Hameau Oger encountered considerable pressure before it stabilised the situation and forced a German withdrawal.

As for 9 Para, its strength was growing all the time as its men continued to arrive in the battalion area after their scattered drop. On the morning of 10 June battalion strength had grown to 270 men and they had adequate supplies. The initial German attack that morning was easily repulsed. The battalion went on to engage some Germans strengthening the Bréville defences and then a German patrol. However, during the morning the enemy reoccupied the Château St-Côme and its outbuildings and infiltrated the wood. Next, in mid-afternoon, a company of

German infantry began to move up each side of the château drive and opened fire with self-propelled guns. Otway's men put up a tenacious defence, but the Germans kept on coming behind a fierce mortar bombardment and it was not until the battalion called for fire support from the *Arethusa* that the attacks were fragmented. The hand-to-hand fighting was bloody and ferocious, but the Germans were eventually stopped and forced to withdraw. Later attempts by the Germans to probe from Sallenelles and Bréville also ground to a halt, but it took a counter-attack by 3 Commando before the front was finally stabilised again.

A Sherman Firefly tank from C Squadron, 13th/18th Hussars, in action near Bréville. *(IWM B5470)*

The situation of 3rd Para Brigade, however, was causing Gale some concern for, as a result of the German attacks and infiltration to the east of DZ N, it had become isolated from the rest of the division. A counter-attack was therefore launched by two companies of 7 Para from the southern edge of DZ N. The attack began in mid-afternoon after B Squadron, 13th/18th Hussars, (eight Shermans with 75-mm guns and a recce troop of five Honey light tanks) had crossed the bridges from the west side

The north-eastern flank.
(Base map: Staff College 1947 tour map)

to add punch to the attack. The aim was to sweep across the southern edge of the drop zone from le Home along the Ranville–le Mariquet–le Mesnil road to the woods in order to effect a junction with 3rd Para Brigade. The attack was a success, the link-up was made and 20 Germans were killed and another 100 taken prisoner. Three Sherman tanks and two Honeys, however, were destroyed by German anti-tank guns in Bréville wood firing on the left flank, leaving the 13th/18th Hussars with ten men dead and two wounded.

The Hussars moved back across the Orne but they were soon to be passed in the opposite direction by 51st (Highland) Division, which was ordered to move over to the east of the Orne during the night by Lt-Gen Crocker, the commander of I Corps, to extend the bridgehead. Maj-Gen Gale immediately began preparations to use one of its battalions against Bréville on the following day. In preparation, Major Ian Dyer led C Company of 9 Para forward to the Château St-Côme, found it empty and occupied it.

10 June was, therefore, an important day in the struggle

The Gordon Highlanders of 51st (Highland) Division approaching the bridges over the Caen Canal and the River Orne on the afternoon of 10 June in order to reinforce 6th Airborne Division that night in the Bois de Bavent. (IWM B5289)

The sunken lane opposite the Château St-Côme driveway was used by the men of 9 Para to get to the bungalow at the Bois du Mont. It was also the start line for the 5th Black Watch attack on Bréville on 11 June. *(Author)*

Château St-Côme viewed from the D37b road to the east. It was from this direction that the Germans launched many attacks against 9 Para. As a result of the attacks Gen Gale decided that the Black Watch would attack from an area to the south of the château and take Bréville. Advancing towards where this photo was taken, the Scottish battalion was cut down in the open fields. *(Author)* for supremacy between the Orne and the Dives, for although it saw the Germans launch another set of major attacks, they were again defeated. With the resources now at his disposal Gale was also in the mood to launch a series of offensives of his own. The first was the successful one along the southern edge of DZ N just described. The second was to be launched on the following day against Bréville which, if taken, would severely damage the German ability to cause trouble in his northern sector and give him full control of the Bavent Ridge.

During the night of 10/11 June, 51st (Highland) Division's 153rd Infantry Brigade passed into 6th Airborne Division's area of operations. In the reorganisation of battalion responsibilities that followed this move, the 1st and 5th/7th Battalions, Gordon Highlanders, took over the southern half of the Bois de Bavent whilst 5th Black Watch moved into an assembly area just south-west of 9 Para in preparation for their assault on Bréville later that morning.

However, in spite of a preliminary bombardment by the guns of the Highland Division and support from the battalion's mortars, the Bréville attack failed. As A Company moved over the open fields in front of Bréville, the leaders were cut down and mortar fire fell on the men following them. The battalion tried to outflank the German positions, but with no success. By 0900 hours A Company consisted of fewer than 30 men, B Company had lost three platoon officers and C Company had a wounded OC and several other casualties. A withdrawal followed and a bloodied Black Watch fell back through 9 Para lines to reorganise in the Bois du Mont before taking up defensive positions around the château.

In the afternoon, the defence around St-Côme was further strengthened by the arrival of three troops of Shermans from the 13th/18th Hussars, but one troop was badly mauled by a self-propelled gun 300 metres to the north of the château and shortly after the other two troops were withdrawn. That night was relatively quiet with just a few German patrols probing the area trying to locate the new British positions, but there were sounds of German vehicles entering Bréville from the east which was the cause of some concern for the British troops in the vicinity.

It was a quiet day for the rest of the division with the focus clearly on Bréville and its immediate surroundings. Even so, the British presence continued to strengthen east of the Orne as

4th Special Service Brigade under Brigadier B.W. Leicester entered the divisional area and came under Gale's command. For the airborne division this support was extremely welcome, but for the Germans, of course, it was ominous.

By 12 June, the Germans were finding it difficult to mount any major attacks to the east of the Orne as their assets had diminished significantly over the previous few days whilst the

Men from 51st (Highland) Division crossing over the Bénouville Bridge on the evening of 10 June. This photo was taken from the west side of the canal looking SE towards LZ X where gliders from the *coup de main* can be seen. *(IWM B5287)*

British presence had increased very markedly. Nevertheless, the day saw the Germans try to dislodge the British for one last time in the area of Bréville. Although it was quiet at the Château St-Côme during the morning, at about noon shelling and mortaring of the British positions began. At 1500 hours it intensified and about 45 minutes later at least a battalion of German infantry, together with six tanks and some self-propelled guns, attacked from the direction of Bréville. The main weight fell on the 5th Black Watch which had taken up positions at the château. Several of its platoons were overrun whilst all of the battalion anti-tank guns were knocked out and nine carriers were hit. During this period the château became the centre of a furious and bloody fight, much of it at close quarters. The British did not crumble, however, and although some ground was given in certain areas, the garrison at the château held on and the Germans were eventually beaten off.

The focus of the fight then moved to 9 Para at the Bois du Mont. Here, too, the fighting was confused and intense as the German tanks and self-propelled guns fired at point-blank range

HISTORY

and the mortar shells dropped mercilessly. The British mortars fired back, as did every other weapon that the battalion had available. With ammunition running short and with darkness about to fall, Otway sent a signal to brigade headquarters asking for help.

The memorial to 9 Para and 5th Black Watch by the driveway to the Château St-Côme. *(Author)*

In response Brigadier Hill personally crossed the le Mesnil road to see if 1 Canadian Para could help reinforce the 9 Para position and found them under attack by German infantry and a couple of tanks from the west. Even so, 60 men were rounded up under Major John Hansen and were led by Hill to the wood south of the château which they successfully cleared. They then pushed up to the château to make sure that the building was firmly held. The arrival of the brigadier and his party certainly increased the morale of the tired troops and by 2000 hours both battalion positions had been secured. Whilst this battle was being fought, Maj-Gen Gale was at le Mesnil and what he saw and heard during his time there convinced him that Bréville had to be taken as soon as possible.

Meanwhile, further south, preparations were being made for an attack on Ste-Honorine and Cuverville on the following day so as to expand the bridgehead southwards as planned. The Highland Division's 152nd Infantry Brigade crossed the Orne late on 12 June in preparation for the attack and deployed in fields between Ranville and le Bas de Ranville (in an area now partly taken up by the Ranville war cemetery). The plan was for 5th Cameron Highlanders to attack Ste-Honorine from Longueval at 0400 hours under cover of a heavy bombardment from the Highland Division's artillery and, this completed, for 6th Seaforth Highlanders, waiting in le Bas de Ranville, to attack Cuverville, while D Company of the Devons moved up onto the Ring Contour in support. By the time that 152nd Brigade arrived just outside Ranville that night, however, events had moved on.

On returning from le Mesnil in the late afternoon, Gale began his preparations for a new attack on Bréville. By 1800 hours he had decided that it would be conducted by the 9 officers and 350 men of 12 Para who were in reserve and the six officers and 80 men of D Company of the Devons who had been preparing to advance with 152nd Brigade the next morning. In support of the attack Gale had negotiated the assistance of a squadron of Shermans from the 13th/18th Hussars and could call on 100 guns from four field regiments and one medium regiment until midnight. As a result it was decided to launch the attack at 2200 hours that evening from the southern edge of Amfréville. When it began there was some confusion as the Devons were still making their final approach to a start line that the Germans were by now shelling heavily. Nevertheless, the attack still proceeded and with the help of the supporting firepower, the German defenders were overwhelmed and the village was taken. British casualties were heavy and included the 12 Para CO, Lt-Col Johnson, who was killed on the start line, and Brigadiers Lovat and Kindersley who were badly wounded by the same shell in Amfréville. However, the expected German counter-attacks did not occur that night or in the morning, and thus the British had won a major prize.

General Gale later said:

'There is a turning point in all battles. In the fight for the Orne bridgehead the Battle of Bréville was that turning point. Neither in the North nor in the South were we ever seriously attacked again. '

Source: R.N. Gale, *With the Sixth Airborne Division in Normandy*.

Wrecked German vehicles in Bréville on 13 June. Two self-propelled guns, a staff car and an anti-aircraft gun can be seen. *(IWM B5473)*

12 June therefore saw the climax to the fighting east of the Orne as the Germans put in one last doomed effort to dislodge the vulnerable troops at St-Côme and the Bois du Mont, and the British hit back to close the Bréville gap for good. Having fought hard for a week, the Germans were a spent offensive force whilst the British, although battered and bruised, had clung onto the vital positions. Although 6th Airborne Division and 1st Special Service Brigade were tired by the end of a full week of fighting and had taken some heavy casualties, reinforcements had ensured that any weaknesses were not terminal and that the left flank of the Allied invasion was finally secured.

CHAPTER 6

6TH AIRBORNE DIVISION IN THE SUMMER OF 1944

6th Airborne Division continued to help to hold the Allied left flank until 16 August, and during this period was not seriously attacked by the Germans. Instead the men spent most of their time consolidating the division's gains. With 1st and 4th Special

Casualties Suffered by 6th Airborne Division

Unit	Killed		Wounded		Missing	
	Off	OR	Off	OR	Off	OR
HQ 6 Airborne Div	4	2	9	13	1	6
Div HQ Defence Platoon	–	3	1	4	–	5
HQ 3 Para Bde & Defence Platoon	4	3	5	26	2	15
1 Canadian Para Battalion	5	60	10	152	4	97
8 Para Battalion	5	73	14	222	3	107
9 Para Battalion	8	54	13	154	2	192
224 Para Field Ambulance	–	9	1	14	3	40
HQ 5 Para Bde & Defence Platoon	–	1	4	18	–	3
7 Para Battalion	6	84	12	236	2	112
12 Para Battalion	4	101	26	387	3	43
13 Para Battalion	3	76	11	215	3	51
225 Para Field Ambulance	–	9	2	17	–	12
22 Indep Para Company	2	6	1	13	1	2
HQ 6 AL Bde & Defence Platoon	1	1	6	18	–	–
12th Devons	4	33	14	212	1	12
2nd Ox & Bucks Light Infantry	9	61	19	238	–	13
1st RUR	6	42	18	217	1	34
195 Airlanding Field Ambulance	–	4	1	14	–	1
HQ, RA	–	1	2	2	–	–
53 Airlanding Light Regt	4	11	2	27	1	1
2 Airlanding LAA Battery	–	–	–	–	–	–
3 Airlanding Anti-Tank Battery	–	10	2	27	–	1
4 Airlanding Anti-Tank Battery	1	12	–	24	3	9
HQ, RE	1	–	2	–	2	1
3 Para Squadron, RE	1	14	2	27	1	1
591 Para Squadron, RE	2	5	3	18	4	16
249 Field Company, RE	–	4	1	36	–	–
286 Field Park Company, RE	1	4	–	3	–	1
CRASC	–	–	–	–	–	–
716 Coy (Airborne Lt Comp)	2	13	1	33	–	9
398 Coy (Airborne Div Comp)	–	7	1	28	–	5
63 Coy (Airborne Div Comp)	–	–	–	6	–	44
HQ REME	–	8	3	8	–	6
Div REME Workshop	–	–	–	–	–	–
Armoured Recce Regt	–	10	6	26	2	8
Div Signals	3	20	7	71	1	21
Div Ordnance Field Park	–	–	–	–	–	–
Div Provost Company	–	4	–	–	1	13
Div Postal Unit	–	–	–	2	–	–
317 Field Security Section	–	–	–	2	–	2
Totals	**76**	**745**	**199**	**2,510**	**41**	**886**

Service Brigades under command, Gale held an area from Sallenelles along the Bavent ridge to approximately 5 km north-west of Troarn with 51st (Highland) Division on the southern flank.

HISTORY

On 15 July General Montgomery visited the division to present decorations for gallantry and, from the Bréville crossroads, looked down onto the Caen plain. It was across this good tank country that Gale had feared a serious German counter-attack, but instead it was the Allied armies which would launch a massive armoured offensive here on 18 July, from the ground that the airborne forces had won. (See the companion volume in this series Battle Zone Normandy: *Battle for Caen*.)

Nevertheless, boredom during this period of static warfare was a real problem for the commanders of these elite troops, who still held the northern perimeter, and intense patrolling and efforts to

A Sherman tank in Herouvillette on 20 July during the breakout from the airborne bridgehead called Operation 'Goodwood'. (IWM B7765)

enlarge the bridgehead did little to assuage this difficulty. On 7 August, however, Lt-Gen Crocker asked Gale to prepare a plan that could be put into action in the event of the enemy withdrawing. Recognising the necessity for this, but hamstrung by the fact that his division did not have the vehicles to make it mobile, the staff had to borrow and improvise what was necessary and on 17 August, Operation 'Paddle', the advance across the Dives, began. This advance, against weakening resistance, was a welcome change for the troops, and by 26 August they had pushed forward all the way to the River Seine. Within a couple of weeks more, however, the men of 6th Airborne Division found themselves back in Bulford. Their Continental adventure, for the time being, was over. Their three months in action had cost them 4,457 casualties: 821 killed, 2,709 wounded and 927 missing.

The 6th Airborne Division did an extremely good job in Normandy. Although many of the frailties of airborne warfare were in evidence, particularly in the earliest moments of the operation, so were many of its strengths and Gale achieved his objectives in just one week. The keys to the division's success were its highly trained and well motivated troops, its first class leaders, its intelligent commanders and a plan that was sympathetic to what airborne warfare could and could not

HISTORY

Ranville War Cemetery during the second week of the invasion. Some graves in the foreground are those of men from 7 Para killed on 10 June. *(IWM B7040)*

achieve. This plan, although demanding, contained objectives that were achievable for lightly armed air-inserted troops by ensuring that the DZs and LZs were close to those objectives and that the division was speedily reinforced by advancing ground forces. Gale's troops defeated all the enemies that they faced and by achieving their mission provided the platform that the Allies required to conduct further offensive operations.

The 13 Para Memorial at Ranville. *(Author)*

PART THREE

BATTLEFIELD TOURS

GENERAL TOURING INFORMATION

Normandy is a thriving holiday area, with some beautiful countryside, excellent beaches and very attractive architecture (particularly in the case of religious buildings). It was also, of course, the scene of heavy fighting in 1944, and this has had a considerable impact on the tourist industry. To make the most of your trip, especially if you intend visiting non-battlefield sites, we strongly recommend you purchase one of the general Normandy guidebooks that are commonly available. These include: *Michelin Green Guide: Normandy*; *Thomas Cook Travellers: Normandy*; *The Rough Guide to Brittany and Normandy*; *Lonely Planet: Normandy*.

TRAVEL REQUIREMENTS

First, make sure you have the proper documentation to enter France as a tourist. Citizens of European Union countries, including Great Britain, should not usually require visas, but will need to carry and show their passports. Others should check with the French Embassy in their own country before travelling. British citizens should also fill in and take Form E111 (available from main post offices), which deals with entitlement to medical treatment, and all should consider taking out comprehensive travel insurance. France is part of the Eurozone, and you should also check exchange rates before travelling.

GETTING THERE

The most direct routes from the UK to Lower Normandy are by ferry from Portsmouth to Ouistreham (near Caen), and from Portsmouth or Poole to Cherbourg. Depending on which you choose, and whether you travel by day or night, the crossing takes between five and seven hours. Alternatively, you can sail to Le Havre, Boulogne or Calais and drive the rest of the way. (Travel time from Calais to Caen is about four hours; motorway

Above: A famous portrait of Maj-Gen Richard 'Windy' Gale outside his headquarters in Ranville on 10 June. *(IWM B5352)*

Page 97: Men from 1st Special Service Brigade on their way to reinforce 6th Airborne Division on the morning of 6 June. *(IWM B5055)*

and bridge tolls may be payable depending on the exact route taken.) Another option is to use the Channel Tunnel. Whichever way you decide to travel, early booking is advised, especially during the summer months.

Although you can of course hire motor vehicles in Normandy, the majority of visitors from the UK or other EU countries will probably take their own. If you do so, you will also need to take: a full driving licence; your vehicle registration document;

The bust of Major John Howard by the Caen Canal. As a young man Howard served in the Shropshire Light Infantry, but left the army in 1938. He re-enlisted in 1939, was commissioned in 1940 and joined the Ox and Bucks Light Infantry. He attained command of D Company in April 1942. *(Author)*

a certificate of motor insurance valid in France (your insurer will advise on this); spare headlight and indicator bulbs; headlight beam adjusters or tape; a warning triangle; and a sticker or number plate identifying which country the vehicle is registered in. Visitors from elsewhere should consult a motoring organisation in their home country for details of the documents and other items they will require.

Normandy's road system is well developed, although there are still a few choke points, especially around the larger towns during rush hour and in the holiday season. As a general guide, in clear conditions it is possible to drive from Cherbourg to Caen in less than two hours.

ACCOMMODATION

Accommodation in Normandy is plentiful and diverse, from cheap campsites to five star hotels in glorious châteaux. However, early booking is advised if you wish to travel between June and August. Useful contacts include:

French Travel Centre, 178 Piccadilly, London W1V 0AL;
   tel: 0870 830 2000; web: www.raileurope.co.uk
Calvados Tourisme, Place du Canada, 14000 Caen;
   tel: +33 (0)2 31 86 53 30; web: www.calvados-tourisme.com
Manche Tourisme; web: www.manchetourisme.com
Maison du Tourisme de Cherbourg et du Haut-Cotentin,
   2 Quai Alexandre III, 50100 Cherbourg-Octeville;
   tel: +33 (0)2 33 93 52 02; web: www.ot-cherbourg-cotentin.fr
Gîtes de France, La Maison des Gîtes de France et du Tourisme
   Vert, 59 rue Saint-Lazare, 75 439 Paris Cedex 09;
   tel: +33 (0)1 49 70 75 75; web: www.gites-de-france.fr

In Normandy itself there are tourist offices in all the large towns and many of the small ones, especially along the coast.

Changes in terrain: The route east out of la Basse Écarde taken by 12 Para and the Devons on 12 June. In 1944 this road was just a rutted track which severely sapped the energy of the British troops moving up for an attack. *(Author)*

BATTLEFIELD TOURING

Each volume in the 'Battle Zone Normandy' series contains from four to six battlefield tours. These are intended to last from a few hours to a full day apiece. Some are best undertaken using motor transport, others should be done on foot, and many involve a mixture of the two. Owing to its excellent infrastructure and relatively gentle topography, Normandy also makes a good location for a cycling holiday; indeed, some of our tours are ideally suited to this method.

In every case the tour author has visited the area concerned recently, so the information presented should be accurate and reasonably up to date. Nevertheless land use, infrastructure and rights of way can change, sometimes at short notice. If you encounter difficulties in following any tour, we would very much like to hear about it, so we can incorporate changes in future editions. Your comments should be sent to the publisher at the address provided at the front of this book.

To derive maximum value and enjoyment from the tours, we suggest you equip yourself with the following items:

BATTLEFIELD TOURS

- Appropriate maps. European road atlases can be purchased from a wide range of locations outside France. However, for navigation within Normandy, the French Institut Géographique National (IGN) produces maps at a variety of scales (www.ign.fr). The 1:100,000 series ('Top 100') is particularly useful when driving over larger distances; sheet 06 (Caen – Cherbourg) covers most of the invasion area. For pinpointing locations precisely, the current IGN 1:25,000 Série Bleue is best (we use extracts from this series for the tour maps in this book). These can be purchased in many places across Normandy. They can also be ordered in the UK from some bookshops, or from specialist dealers such as the Hereford Map Centre, 24–25 Church Street, Hereford HR1 2LR; tel: 01432 266322; web: <www.themapcentre.com>. Allow at least a fortnight's notice, although some maps may be in stock.
- Lightweight waterproof clothing and robust footwear are essential, especially for touring in the countryside.
- Take a compass, provided you know how to use one!
- A camera and spare films/memory cards.
- A notebook to record what you have photographed.
- A French dictionary and/or phrasebook. (English is widely spoken in the coastal area, but is much less common inland.)

Gliders of 6th Airlanding Brigade on the afternoon of 6 June just a few hours before they took off from RAF Harwell. The glider on the far left bears the chalk number 151 which reveals it as one of the six Horsas of 195 Airlanding Field Ambulance, destined for LZ W. *(IWM H39176)*

Part of the 6th Airlanding Brigade air armada on the evening of 6 June at RAF Tarrant Rushton. The tugs are all Halifax bombers and most of the gliders are Hamilcars with two Horsas at the front of the queue on the runway. *(IWM CL76)*

- Food and drink. Although you are never very far in Normandy from a shop, restaurant or *tabac*, many of the tours do not pass directly by such facilities. It is therefore sensible to take some light refreshment with you.
- Binoculars. Most officers and some other ranks carried binoculars in 1944. Taking a pair adds a surprising amount of verisimilitude to the touring experience.

SOME DO'S AND DON'TS

Battlefield touring can be an extremely interesting and even emotional experience, especially if you have read something about the battles beforehand. In addition, it is fair to say that residents of Normandy are used to visitors, among them battlefield tourists, and generally will do their best to help if you encounter problems. However, many of the tours in the 'Battle Zone Normandy' series are off the beaten track, and you can expect some puzzled looks from the locals, especially inland. In all cases we have tried to ensure that tours are on public land, or viewable from public rights of way. However, in the unlikely event that you are asked to leave a site, do so immediately and by the most direct route.

In addition: **Never remove 'souvenirs' from the battlefields.** Even today it is not unknown for farmers to turn up relics of the 1944 fighting. Taking these without permission may not only be

A view towards Cuverville and the Caen Plain from the Ring Contour. This position provided valuable observation over the good tank country on the British southern flank, but was also extremely exposed to German fire. It was over this ground that Operation 'Goodwood' was launched in July 1944. *(Author)*

illegal, but can be extremely dangerous. It also ruins the site for genuine battlefield archaeologists. Anyone returning from France should also remember customs regulations on the import of weapons and ammunition of any kind.

Be especially careful when investigating fortifications. Some of the more frequently-visited sites are well preserved, and several of them have excellent museums. However, both along the coast and inland there are numerous positions that have been left to decay, and which carry risks for the unwary. In particular, remember that many of these places were the scenes of heavy fighting or subsequent demolitions, which may have caused severe (and sometimes invisible) structural damage. Coastal erosion has also undermined the foundations of a number of shoreline defences. Under no circumstances should underground bunkers, chambers and tunnels be entered, and care should always be taken when examining above-ground structures. If in any doubt, stay away.

Beware of hunting (shooting) areas (signposted *Chasse Gardée*). Do not enter these, even if they offer a short cut to your destination. Similarly, Normandy contains a number of restricted areas (military facilities and wildlife reserves), which should be avoided. Watch out, too, for temporary footpath closures, especially along sections of coastal cliffs.

If using a motor vehicle, keep your eyes on the road. There are many places to park, even on minor routes, and it is always better to turn round and retrace your path than to cause an accident. In rural areas avoid blocking entrances and driving along farm tracks; again, it is better to walk a few hundred metres than to cause damage and offence.

In addition various points specific to this volume should be raised. The best detailed maps of the area discussed in this book are the IGN Série Bleue sheets *16120T Caen* and *1612E Dives-sur-Mer – Cabourg*.

It is important to note that, although much of the countryside of the Orne Bridgehead is still very similar to that encountered by the troops in June 1944, it is inevitable that towns and village have grown (and often merged), many of the tracks have become roads, and some of the minor roads have become much more substantial. In addition, in the southern part of the battlefield in particular there are far more trees, bushes and hedges than there were during the invasion, but in most other areas there has been a clearance of the same. It is clearly important, therefore, to try to imagine what the landscape might have looked like to the men who fought in the area (hopefully the contemporary photographs and maps will help in this) with few buildings, fewer cars, less substantial roads and generally more greenery. It is still possible, however, to work out how the area must have looked back in 1944 without too much difficulty whilst standing on the ground.

Please be careful that you park your car in a sensible place, be vigilant whilst walking along the roads and lanes and be careful, if you do wander off the beaten track, that you are not damaging valuable crops or trespassing. If in doubt about the access to a certain site, always try to talk to the farmer first. We have never been refused permission to explore private land and on many occasions have found the farmer to be knowledgeable, friendly and indulgent with his wine!

WIDER MILITARY TOURISM

There are numerous museums (of variable quality) relating to the Battle of Normandy close to the Orne Bridgehead area. The two relating directly to the material in this book are highlighted in the tour section below, but the following are also worth visiting: *Le Mémorial de Caen*, Esplanade Eisenhower, Caen; tel: +33 (0)2 31 06 06 44; web: <www.memorial-caen.fr>; *Musée No 4 Commando*, Place Alfred Thomas, 14150 Ouistreham; *Musée du Débarquement*, Place du 6 Juin, 14117 Arromanches;

tel: +33 (0)2 31 22 34 31; web: <www.normandy1944.com>; *Musée le Mur de l'Atlantique*, Avenue du 6 Juin, 14150 Ouistreham/Riva Bella; tel: +33 (0)2 31 97 28 69 email: <bunkermusée@aol.com>; *Musée America Gold Beach*, 2 Place Admiral Byrd, 14114 Ver-Sur-Mer; tel: +33 (0)2 31 22 58 58; web: <www.normandy-tourism.org>.

WIDER GENERAL TOURISM

Normandy is not, of course, just an old battlefield but a place packed with historic buildings, museums and other stimulating attractions. The following are merely a flavour of all that is on offer: *Musée de Normandie*; tel: +33 (0)2 31 30 47 60; email: <mdn@ville-caen.fr>; web: <www.ville-caen.fr/mdn>, is a museum tracing the history of Normandy from pre-history to the present day; *Beaux-Arts Museum*, tel: +33 (0)2 31 30 47 70, is Caen's fine art museum; *Le Musée d'Initiation à la Nature*,

Taken on 15 June in Herouvillette, this photograph shows three men from the D Company, 2 OBLI, glider *coup de main* force on the bridges over the Caen Canal and River Orne. From left to right they are Private Frank Gardener, Captain Brian Priday (the company second-in-command who landed near Varaville) and Lance-Corporal B.H. Lambley. *(IWM B5586)*

tel: +33 (0)2 31 30 43 27, covers the region's fauna, flora and countryside; and for children (although there is also plenty to occupy adults) *Parc Festyland*, Route de Caumont-Bretteville/ Odon; tel: +33 (0)2 31 75 04 04; web: <www.festyland.com>; email: <festyland@festyland.com>; which combines culture, sport and a theme park.

For up to date information about local facilities, places to stay and special events consult the *Office de Tourisme de Caen*, Place Sainte Pierre, F–14000 Caen; tel: +33 (0)2 31 27 14 14; email: <tourisminfo@ville-caen.fr>; web: <www.ville-caen.fr>.

The directions given in the tours described below assume that tourers will begin from Caen, which is of course easily accessible from wherever in the region visitors may be staying.

TOUR A

PEGASUS BRIDGE – HORSA BRIDGE

OBJECTIVE: A tour of the area attacked by Major John Howard's glider borne *coup de main* force in the early hours of 6 June 1944.

DURATION/SUITABILITY: Half a day (walking or by car, including a visit to the museum). Suitable for cyclists and the disabled.

APPROACH TO BATTLE: D Company, 2nd Oxfordshire and Buckinghamshire Light Infantry, had been prepared superbly well by their commander, Major John Howard, in preparation for their crucial Normandy mission. Once chosen as the *coup de main* force by virtue of their excellence, Howard's men were separated from the rest of the battalion and undertook special training, using whatever resources they required. Mistakes were made during this period, but many valuable lessons were also learned. Indeed, as Howard was told more about his objectives, he asked for and received two extra platoons of men from

BATTLEFIELD TOURS

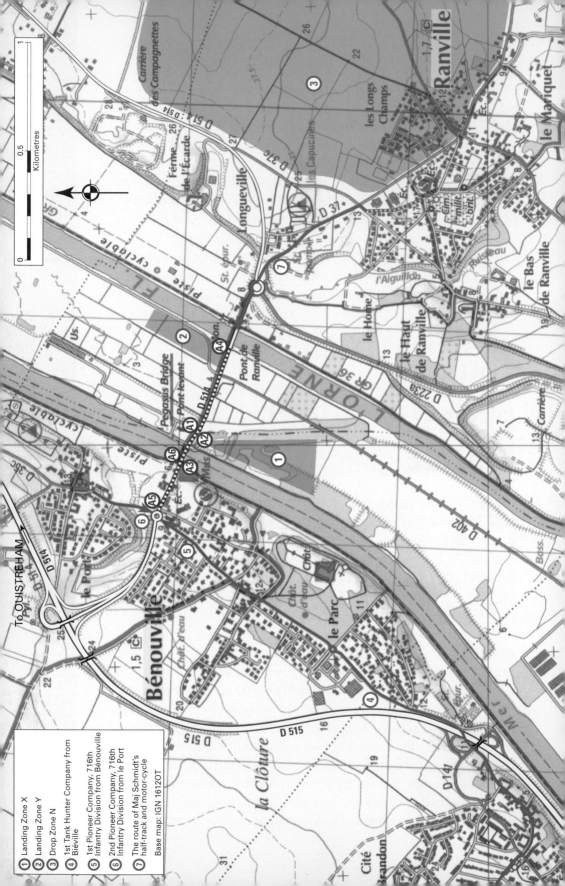

To OUISTREHAM

Bénouville

Ranville

le Mariquet

le Bas de Ranville

le Haut de Ranville

le Home

l'Aiguillon

les Longs Champs

les Capucines

Longueville

Ferme de l'Écarde

Carrière des Campagnettes

Pegasus Bridge

Pont-levant

Pont de Ranville

L'ORNE

le Parc

la Clôture

Cité Brandon

① Landing Zone X
② Landing Zone Y
③ Drop Zone N
④ 1st Tank Hunter Company from Biéville
⑤ 1st Pioneer Company, 716th Infantry Division from Bénouville
⑥ 2nd Pioneer Company, 716th Infantry Division from le Port
⑦ The route of Maj Schmidt's half-track and motor-cycle

Base map: IGN 1612OT

Kilometres

D 514
D 37c
D 37
D 223
D 402
D 515
D 141

The Pegasus Bridge sign now at the western end of the bridge is a replica. The original (held by the *Mémorial Pegasus*) was unveiled on 26 June 1944. *(Author)*

B Company and 30 sappers. The glider pilots, who had the crucial task of landing the flimsy contraptions as close as possible to the objectives, also underwent intensive training. Flying in all weathers by day and during the night, in time they learned to land on small triangular LZs from a release height of 6,000 ft (1,800 m). Nothing was left to chance. In May the latest intelligence from the area was scrutinised, the training became as realistic as possible and the plan was fine-tuned. It was only when the company was sealed in its concentration area at RAF Tarrant Rushton in Dorset, however, that Howard's men were fully briefed about the airborne operation and their part in it. When Maj Gen Gale gave his briefing to the men just a few days before their departure he said, 'the German today is like the June bride. He knows he is going to get it, but he doesn't know how big it is going to be.' During the final days more briefings took place and the men re-checked their equipment – each man weighed 250 pounds instead of the allotted 210 pounds – but they were ready to go.

Stand A1: Mémorial Pegasus

DIRECTIONS: Bénouville, where this tour begins, is situated on the west bank of the Caen Canal between Caen and Ouistreham. From Caen take the D515 heading northwards to Bénouville where you will meet the D514 (which is the road south from Ouistreham). Join the D514 which turns east at Bénouville to cross the canal and the Orne. The *Mémorial* is on the left immediately after you cross the canal and has a car park.

THE SITE: The *Mémorial*, a fine modern museum, is a good place to begin any exploration of the 6th Airborne Division's area of operations in Normandy. The airy main building tells the story

> ## Mémorial Pegasus
>
> *Mémorial Pegasus*, Avenue du Major Howard, 14860 Ranville;
> tel: +33 (0)2 31 78 19 44; fax: +33 (0)2 31 78 19 42;
> email: <memorial.pegasus@wanadoo.fr>; web: <www.normandy1944.com>.
> Museum open 0930–1830 May–Sept, 1000–1300 and 1400–1700 Oct–Nov
> and Feb–Apr, closed Dec and Jan. Admission charge; parking. There is a gift
> shop and lavatories, but no café.

of the division's actions in Normandy and the adjacent park contains wonderful exhibits including the original Pegasus Bridge (which was replaced in the winter of 1993 by a stronger bridge better able to cope with heavy modern traffic), a Bailey Bridge and (a new exhibit) a replica Horsa Glider.

STAND A2: The Pegasus Bridge Gliders

DIRECTIONS: Turn right out of the *Mémorial Pegasus*. On the opposite side of the road just before the bridge, a path leads off on the left – the Esplanade Major John Howard. Stand by the 50-mm anti-tank gun still mounted in its Tobruk pit (but moved a few metres from its original position when the canal here was widened in 1994). Looking left down the canal, in 1944 there was a line of trees running along the side of the canal towpath. In this area there was another pill-box, which doubled as the garrison HQ for the bridge defences, and between the towpath and the canal were slit trenches and weapons pits. From the anti-tank gun, turn around and walk down the path leading into the field adjacent to the canal. Here there is a bronze bust of Major Howard by Vivien Mallock which was presented to the mayor and people of Bénouville by the Airborne Assault Normandy Trust and the Ox and Bucks LI Association in 1994. Individual markers have been placed in the vicinity of where each of the three assaulting gliders on LZ X landed.

THE ACTION: At 2256 hours on 5 June 1944, three Halifax bombers from 644 Squadron and three from 298 Squadron began taking off, one minute apart, from RAF Tarrant Rushton towing six Horsa gliders carrying Howard's six infantry platoons (with attached engineers) to Normandy. The flight over to France was calm and the gliders were released over the Normandy coast at 6,000 feet (1,830 metres), the noise made by the engines of the

Pegasus Bridge and the Esplanade Major John Howard from the landing position of Glider No. 93 which broke in two. It was on this spot that Lieutenant Smith and Captain Vaughan were thrown through the cockpit of the aircraft, together with an unfortunate soldier who drowned in the adjacent pond. *(Author)*

tug aircraft being masked by those of other aircraft on their way to bomb Caen. The lead glider, No. 91, was piloted by Staff Sergeants Wallwork and Ainsworth and contained Howard and 23 men of Lieutenant Den Brotheridge's No. 1 Platoon, plus five sappers from 249 Field Company, Royal Engineers. The weather was warm but although the moon was full it was obscured by clouds being hurried along by a strong wind. After casting off, the gliders were flown by stopwatch, compass, airspeed and altimeter. They glided silently southwards to the east of the Caen Canal and then turned right and then right again to head north to LZ X at 500 feet and 110 mph (150 metres and 175 km/hr).

The original Pegasus Bridge in the grounds of the *Mémorial Pegasus*. Built in 1933, it was replaced in 1993 by a modern structure. After lying in a nearby field for several years, the bridge was moved to its present location in 2000 where it was renovated in time for the inauguration of the Mémorial by Prince Charles on 4 June that year. *(Author)*

Wallwork could see nothing in the darkness, but at 0014 hours he shouted to Howard to get ready and the men linked arms and brought their knees up in preparation for the landing. Around 90 seconds later the clouds parted enough for Wallwork to see his LZ. The glider was travelling at 100 mph and at altitude of 200 feet (160 km/hr and 60 metres) during this final approach.

All was quiet at the bridge. The commander of the 50-man German garrison of largely Eastern European troops from 736th Grenadier Regiment of 716th Infantry Division, was *Major* Hans Schmidt. Schmidt was not anxious about an Allied invasion that night because of the blustery weather and so he was in Ranville with his girlfriend. Indeed, he had even failed to put the demolition charges into their chambers on the bridge in case they were accidentally set off or were sabotaged by members of the French Resistance. This lackadaisical attitude was infectious and was easily passed on to his men who went about their routine without fear of imminent attack. There were two young German sentries on the Bénouville Bridge that night; one of them, a 16-year old called Helmut Romer, heard Allied bombers hammering Caen, but that was not unusual.

As glider No. 91 touched down on the 300 metre long LZ at 80 mph (130 km/hr), Ainsworth deployed the arrester parachute which slowed the aircraft, but also lifted the tail and pushed the nose wheel down. The glider bounced into the air again and all three wheels were torn off. The parachute was then jettisoned and the glider slowed to around 100 km/hr and hit the ground again with a shower of sparks as the skids hit rocks and stones – then there was a crash. The two pilots were thrown through the Perspex cockpit windscreen whilst still strapped to their seats and knocked unconscious, as were the men inside.

Denis Edwards, a private in D Company, 2 OBLI, remembered that:

'No one stirred, nothing moved. My immediate thought was, "God help me – we must all be dead." ...Then some of the others began to stir and the realisation that we were not all dead came quickly as bodies began unstrapping themselves and moving around in the darkness of the glider's shattered interior.'

Source: Denis Edwards, *The Devil's Own Luck.*

Two of the three gliders that landed so close to the canal bridge. In front is the broken glider No. 93, which carried Lieutenant Wood's platoon. Behind is glider No. 91 (Lieutenant Brotheridge's platoon) which crashed into the defensive wire strung out around the east end of the bridge. The trees hide the bridge, but the *Café Gondrée* can be seen in the left rear of the photo. *(IWM B5233)*

The glider had smashed through the perimeter wire of the bridge at the exact spot that Howard had wanted – just 50 metres from the eastern end of the bridge.

The Germans on the bridge heard the crash and dismissed it as parts of Allied aircraft falling to the ground having been hit by German AA guns – a not uncommon occurrence. Meanwhile, the dazed airborne soldiers extracted themselves from the glider and formed up for their attack. Brotheridge sent Private Bailey and two others to destroy the pill-box at the eastern end of the bridge while he led the assault across the bridge.

Glider No. 93 on LZ X on 12 June. This photograph clearly shows how the glider broke in two as the pilot tried to swerve to avoid a crash with glider No. 91. Three men were thrown through the cockpit and out of the glider as it came to a sudden halt: the platoon commander, Lieutenant Smith; the MO, Captain John Vaughan; and a private who drowned in the pond. *(IWM B7036)*

Howard watched the platoon move off just as the second glider, No. 92, piloted by Staff Sergeants Boland and Hobbs, carrying Lieutenant David Wood's No. 2 Platoon, landed and stopped just short of the pond. As the sentries crossed in the middle of the bridge, Romer spotted the attackers, turned and ran shouting '*Fallschirmjäger* [paratroops]!' at the other sentry as he passed him. The second sentry pulled out a signal pistol and fired a flare into the night sky just as Brotheridge cut him down with his Sten. Meanwhile, Bailey's party shoved grenades into the slits

The Esplanade Major John Howard, with two of the glider landing markers, looking south. The pond can be seen on the left but the Caen Canal is out of shot on the right. This photograph is taken from where a minor earth bank used to be which had to be passed over before getting to the end of the bridge and the German defences. *(Author)*

of the pill box, and then ran across the bridge to take up positions near the *Café Gondrée* at the west end. As they did so, the sappers crawled over the bridge and cut wires and fuses. Romer's shout, the flare and the explosion in the pill-box woke up the men in the weapons pits who began edging away. The NCOs, however, all of whom were German, opened fire with their MG 34s and sub-machine guns. Brotheridge was nearly across the bridge and had just thrown a grenade at a machine-gun position on his right when he was hit in the neck by a bullet and collapsed to the ground. Private Billy Gray was following firing a Bren gun from his hip. Brotheridge's grenade went off and silenced the machine gun on the right; Gray and others knocked out a second machine gun before clearing the underground bunkers to the left.

Minutes later Wood's platoon arrived at the eastern end of the bridge and began clearing the trenches in the area. As they did so the third glider, No. 93, flown by Staff Sergeants Barkaway and Boyle, carrying Lieutenant Sandy Smith's No. 3 Platoon, touched down and, in a desperate attempt not to collide with No. 91, swerved towards the pond, ripping the tail off. Smith was thrown past the two pilots in the crash and landed in front of the glider badly spraining his knee; another man was also flung through the cockpit and drowned in the pond and the Medical Officer, Captain John Vaughan, was hurled out and lay unconscious whilst the platoon attacked the west end of the bridge.

STAND A3: Café Gondrée

DIRECTIONS: Cross the bridge and at the western end on the immediate left is the famous *Café Gondrée*. There is a car park for patrons adjacent to the café and a public one next to that. This has a good claim to be the first building in France to be liberated by the Allies and contains a little museum, a souvenir shop and a briefing room.

The café is usually closed between the last week in November and the first week in March. Information about the café and its facilities can be obtained from M. Gondrée-Pritchett, tel/fax: +33 (0)2 31 44 62 25.

Adjacent to the café is the Pegasus Bridge signpost which is a copy, renovated in 2003. The original (now held in the Mémorial Pegasus) was designed and made in the workshops of 286 Field Park Company, RE, here in June 1944 after the bridge had been renamed by the airborne troops and was unveiled on 26 June 1944. Opposite the *Café Gondrée* is *Les 3 Planeurs* café-restaurant with an A27M Centaur tank on display outside – this type was used by the Royal Marine Commando Armoured Support Unit. This specimen was recovered from Sword Beach at la Brèche d'Hermanville and was restored and placed here in 1975.

THE ACTION: Lieutenant Smith struggled across to the western end of the bridge but was wounded again in the wrist when a German stick grenade went off beside him by the *Café Gondrée*. Nevertheless, he continued to lead his platoon in mopping up the resistance from the machine-gun pits and trenches.

> **Lieutenant Sandy Smith later said:**
>
> 'The poor buggers in the bunkers didn't have much of a chance and we were not taking any prisoners or messing around, we just threw phosphorous grenades down and high-explosive grenades into the dug-outs there and anything that moved we shot.'
>
> *Source:* Carl Shiletto, *Pegasus Bridge & Merville Battery.*

The *Café Gondrée* at the western end of Pegasus bridge. This original building was home to the Gondrée family in 1944. M. Gondrée provided valuable intelligence about the bridge defences to the British via the local Resistance organisation. The café was to be Lieutenant Brotheridge's headquarters after the seizing of the bridge but he was killed before reaching the building. M. Gondrée celebrated the liberation of his home by digging up 98 bottles of champagne which he had hidden in his back garden and many airborne troops enjoyed a drink there during the first few days of the battle when it was being used as a first aid post. (*Author*)

As the western end of the bridge fell to D Company, Wood's platoon was mopping up at the other end, clearing the slit trenches and the bunkers as most of the enemy ran away. As his men occupied the slit trenches vacated by the Germans, Wood went to report his success to Howard at his command post in a trench adjacent to the pill-box, but when approaching the position he was hit by three bullets in his leg by a stray German, who also wounded Wood's runner and his platoon sergeant.

By 0021 hours the three platoons at the bridge had subdued most of the resistance from the enemy and Captain Jack Neilson, commander of the sappers, gave Howard the news that the bridge was clear of explosives. Although relieved that the Bénouville bridge had been taken, Howard soon learned that all three of his platoon commanders had been wounded and he still awaited news from the Ranville bridge party.

Stand A4: Horsa Bridge

DIRECTIONS: Walk east from Pegasus Bridge along the D514 towards Ranville or 'Horsa' bridge as the airborne forces dubbed it. Note the track on the left after 150 metres, discussed later in this section. As you approach the Ranville bridge there is a memorial on the left and the field behind it is LZ Y, where gliders No. 95 and 96 landed.

LZ Y where gliders containing platoons commanded by Lieutenants Fox and Sweeney landed. Both landed in the field behind the trees that now mask the view. *(Author)*

Horsa Bridge looking east towards Ranville. This structure is not the original Eiffel bridge which was removed in 1971. There were no defences at the end of the bridge from which the photo was taken, but there were machine-gun positions on the bank that rises up to meet the road on the other side. *(Author)*

THE ACTION: As the fight at Pegasus Bridge was starting, the gliders attacking the bridge over the River Orne came in to land. At the east end of the bridge there were two open machine gun posts on the north side of the road and on the southern side of the road a camouflaged pill-box, but there were no defences at the western end. The first glider that was due to land on LZ Y, glider No. 94, piloted by Staff Sergeants Lawrence and Shorter, actually landed near Varaville at a bridge over the Divette owing to a navigational error. As a result Lieutenant Tony Hooper's No. 4 Platoon and D Company's second-in-command, Captain Brian Priday, found themselves some 13 km off target. Staff Sergeants Howard and Baacke piloted glider No. 96, containing Lieutenant Dennis Fox's No. 6 Platoon, and they were the first to land on LZ Y (although they should have been the third), stopping approximately 300 metres from the bridge. As a result of the fighting at the Bénouville bridge, the sentries were on full alert and a machine gun opened up on them as Fox led his men forward. As the platoon dived for cover, Sergeant 'Wagger' Thornton had anticipated this German reaction and let loose with a 2-inch mortar round which destroyed the German position. With this the platoon charged forward and the remaining German sentries ran away in the direction of Ranville

A view looking west towards Pegasus Bridge from Horsa Bridge. The distance is short, but it was some considerable time before Howard knew for certain that his men had taken the bridge over the Orne. *(Author)*

leaving the British to turn their abandoned MG 34 on them as they fled. Fox's platoon then spread out as sappers worked on removing detonation wires and searching for explosives but, as on the Canal bridge, the chambers were empty.

One minute after Fox's platoon had landed, glider No. 95, piloted by Staff Sergeants Pearson and Guthrie and containing Lieutenant Tod Sweeney's No. 5 Platoon, touched down about 700 metres short of the bridge. On nearing the objective with his men Sweeney became worried by the quiet and, not knowing that the bridge had already been taken, left one section on the bank of the river, and moved the other two sections forward to attack across the bridge. It was not until Fox stood up and came forward from the eastern end that Sweeney realised what had happened.

As at Bénouville the attack had seized the Ranville bridge in just minutes, and in this case with hardly a shot being fired. The months of intensive training had paid off. There had been glitches, but they had been overcome and D Company, 2 OBLI, and the glider pilots had made an extremely difficult task look very easy.

At approximately 0026 hours Howard received the message from Sweeney that the bridge over the Orne had been taken and with considerable relief transmitted the two prearranged code words, 'Ham and Jam', informing 5th Para Brigade HQ and the relieving force, 7 Para, of his success.

As a result of the activity at the bridges, including the ambush of a German patrol on the east side of the River Orne, *Major* Schmidt set off from Ranville in an open half-track with his driver, and a motor-cycle following, to find out what was happening. The motor-cycle and its rider were hit by troops at the east end of the Ranville bridge and the half-track drove into a hail of fire at the west end and ran off the road.

Both Schmidt and his driver were badly wounded and were taken on stretchers to the OBLI's regimental aid post, which had been set up between the two bridges. (The RAP was on the lane to the side of the D514, as described above.) By this time Vaughan had regained consciousness after being thrown out of the glider and had ministered to all of Howard's platoon commanders from Bénouville bridge, although Brotheridge had died shortly afterwards. Schmidt's 16-year-old driver was also too badly injured to save, but Schmidt himself, says Vaughan, was:

> '... sufficiently able to forget about the wound in his leg to harangue me about the futility of this Allied attempt to defeat the master race. We were undoubtedly going to end up in the sea he assured me with complete conviction... He ended his lecture by requesting me to shoot him. This I did – in the bottom – with a needle attached to a syringe of morphia. The effect of this, it seemed, induced him to take a more reasonable view of things and in about ten minutes he actually thanked me for my medical attentions.'

Source: John Vaughan, *All Spirits.*

BATTLEFIELD TOURS

Stand A5: Bénouville T-junction

DIRECTIONS: Walk 250 metres into Bénouville from Pegasus Bridge to the small roundabout, which has replaced the T-junction that was here back in 1944. Stand next to the 7 Para Memorial to the right in the Place de la Libération. To the left is the town hall, the first to be liberated by the Allies in France, with a plaque by the front door to commemorate the fact. In front of the building is a monument to the fallen of the First World War; this was damaged by the fighting in June 1944.

A view from the former T-junction down to Pegasus Bridge. It was on this spot that Sergeant Thornton stopped a German tank with his PIAT at 0130 hours on 6 June. *(Author)*

THE ACTION: D Company had to reorganise quickly for its defence of the bridges as Howard knew that the Germans were likely to counter-attack as soon they could. Thus, he ordered Sweeney to hold the Ranville bridge whilst Fox moved his platoon across the Bénouville bridge and up to the junction with the road linking Bénouville with le Port. Howard's priority was to place his defensive weight at the bridge over the Caen Canal as he knew there would not be any friendly troops to the west for many hours, while 5th Para Brigade would be landing to the east within the half hour. As the transfer was taking place German tank engines could be heard coming from Bénouville and le Port and so a PIAT, the only anti-tank weapon available to the company, was put in the hands of Sergeant Thornton as he approached the junction.

As Fox's men were digging in, the sound of 5th Para Brigade's air armada was heard overhead, but D Company at the bridges understood that it would still be some considerable time before they were relieved by 7 Para. As the aircraft dropped the main body of parachutists on DZ N, Brigadier Poett, who had landed with the advance party, met Howard at his command post.

Brigadier J.E.N. Poett, commander of 5th Para Brigade receiving the DSO. Poett was a regular officer from the Durham Light Infantry who took command of the brigade in 1943. *(IWM BU4747)*

Brigadier Poett describes his landing on 6 June:

'I was very well dropped. When I landed, it was absolute and complete blackness. There was not a soul in sight and not a sound apart from the noise of the aircraft going away. I could see the exhausts of the aircraft and knew the direction in which they were flying, which was towards

Ranville. I moved up in the line in the direction in which they were heading, and met a private soldier from my defence platoon. A few seconds later, the attack on the bridges went in and we could see the flashes and hear the sounds. I immediately headed for the bridges, not waiting for anyone else, where I expected to meet my wireless operator who was an officer. Unfortunately, he had been killed on the DZ.'

Source: Peter Harclerode, *Go To It! The Illustrated History of the 6th Airborne Division.*

As Poett and Howard talked, engines could be heard moving towards Fox's position. Within moments two armoured vehicles came into view from Bénouville and the first turned slowly right at the T-junction and began moving towards the bridge. Probably from 1st Tank Hunter Company, which had rushed to the area from Biéville, they were followed by engineers from 716th Infantry Division billeted in Bénouville village and le Port. What these troops lacked was information and so, foolishly, they groped forward with their armour. Thornton held his fire until he knew that the vehicle was in range, pulled the trigger, hit the vehicle right in the middle and watched as it burst into flames. Thinking that the British had anti-tank guns with them at the bridges, the Germans decided to wait till dawn to clarify the situation and withdrew.

Major Hans von Luck, 125th Panzergrenadier Regiment, about his desire to respond to the airborne landings:

'My idea was, after I got more information about the parachute landings, and the gliders, was that a night attack would be the right way to counter-attack, starting at three o'clock or four o'clock in the morning, before the British could organise their defences, before their air force people could come, before the British Navy could hit us. We were quite familiar with the ground and I think that we could have been able to get through to the bridges.'

Source: Stephen Ambrose, *Pegasus Bridge.*

7 Para, meanwhile, had been scattered during its drop and when it left the rendezvous at 0230 hours was only at half strength. The battalion eventually linked up with Howard's men

at around 0300 hours and immediately crossed both bridges. A Company set up its defences around the houses in the southern part of Bénouville; B Company established itself in le Port and the woods nearby; and C Company set up an outpost at Château de Bénouville in the south and another at the bend in the canal 1.5 km to the north.

The 7 Para Memorial at the former T-junction in Bénouville with the *mairie* (town hall) in the background on the left. Although 7 Para held this area on the morning of 6 June, it was still extremely dangerous when 1st Special Service Brigade moved through in the early afternoon. *(Author)*

Stand A6: Consolidation at Pegasus Bridge

DIRECTIONS: Walk back to Pegasus Bridge. Just by the *Café Gondrée* car park is a memorial to 1st Special Service Brigade. This commemorates the commando link-up with the airborne forces, at 1202 hours and 30 seconds (local time).

THE ACTION: As dawn broke, German activity in Bénouville and le Port developed and snipers in particular made it dangerous to move about near the Caen Canal. As the morning progressed, Lt-Col Pine-Coffin's under-strength 7 Para came under increasing pressure as it was attacked by German infantry, armour and self-propelled guns and was forced to give ground as significant

An Army Photographic Intelligence image of the bridges over the Caen Canal and River Orne on the morning of 6 June. Major John Howard's five gliders are visible as is the western extremity of DZ/LZ N. *(IWM MH24891)*

casualties were taken. Nevertheless, as soon as the beach invasion started, the parachutists fought on in the morale-boosting knowledge that 1st Special Service Brigade was endeavouring to link up with them. At 0900 hours Gale, Kindersley and Poett all turned up at the Bénouville bridge on their way to Pine-Coffin's headquarters, marching in step, with their red berets firmly planted on their heads, refusing to flinch as German small arms fire lashed around them. Soon after Howard was ordered to send a platoon over the bridge to assist A Company in Bénouville and by midday, with most of the 7 Para stragglers having found their way to the battalion, the situation had stabilised.

Less than an hour later the sound of bagpipes was heard coming from St-Aubin and at around 1300 hours Piper Bill Millin and Brigadier Lord Lovat came into view, accompanied by a Churchill tank, and leading 1st Special Service Brigade into le Port. The commandos immediately crossed the Bénouville Bridge with 45 Commando first and 3 Commando immediately behind them. As the bridge was still under fire a number of casualties were taken, including Lt-Col N.C. Ries commanding 45 Commando, but they continued to move swiftly towards their objectives at Hameau Oger, le Plain and Amfréville.

During mid-afternoon the German counter-attacks to the west of the canal were contained as 7 Para began to win back some of the ground that had been lost earlier in the day. The fighting, however, continued and it was a great relief to Pine-Coffin when his relieving force, 2nd Battalion, The Royal Warwickshire Regiment, arrived in le Port that evening. The hand-over to the Warwicks was a rather protracted affair but, when it was completed close to midnight, 7 Para marched back over the bridges to a reserve position on the western edge of the DZ. The day had been successful, but it cost the battalion 60 casualties.

TOUR B

THE MERVILLE BATTERY

OBJECTIVE: A tour of the attack conducted by 9 Para on the Merville Battery from their drop zone through to their objective on the morning of 6 June 1944.

DURATION/SUITABILITY: Half a day (including a visit to the museum) if in a car. Suitable for cyclists and the disabled.

BATTLEFIELD TOURS

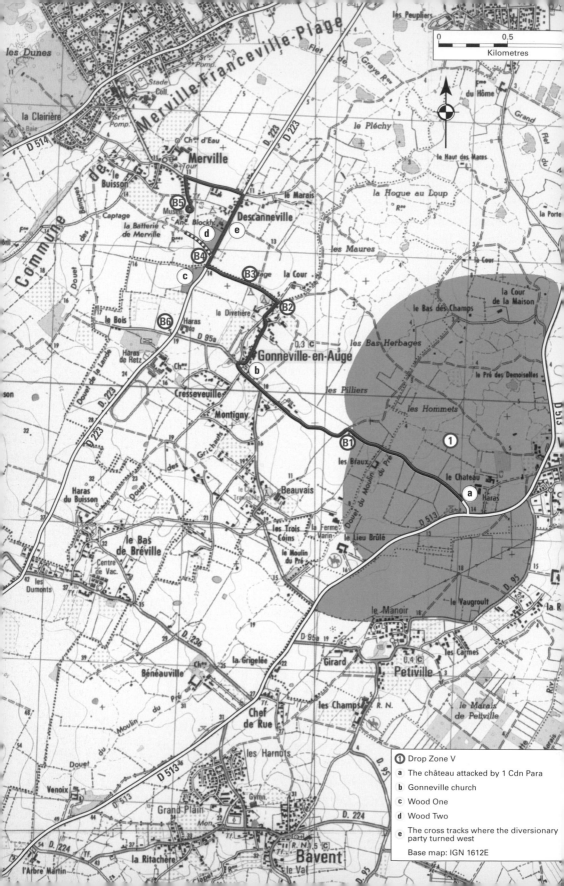

① Drop Zone V

a The château attacked by 1 Cdn Para

b Gonneville church

c Wood One

d Wood Two

e The cross tracks where the diversionary party turned west

Base map: IGN 1612E

APPROACH TO BATTLE: 9 Para was not an experienced battalion but in the months before the invasion of Normandy the men worked extremely hard from their base at Bulford Camp to do everything they could to ready themselves for their coming challenges. The first objective that Lt-Col Otway's men were given was the neutralisation of the guns at the heavily defended coastal battery at Merville that was believed to threaten the landings at Sword Beach. The guns here were protected by four casemates which were set in an arc facing north-west and protected to the west by an anti-tank ditch 300 metres long, 5 metres wide and 3 metres deep. A belt of barbed wire 1.5 metres high and 5 metres deep protected the battery, including the area of the anti-tank ditch, and on the eastern side there were two further belts of wire and a cattle fence. The distance between this outer cattle fence and the dense inner belts was between 80 and 160 metres and contained a minefield of anti-tank and anti-personnel mines. Inside the battery there were more barbed wire obstacles together with weapons pits, trenches, machine-gun positions, 20-mm dual-purpose AA guns and a garrison of some 160 men from 1st Battery, 1716th Artillery Regiment.

Confronted with such a daunting task Otway said, 'The basis of my plan was surprise and the fact that I did not intend to allow the garrison to concentrate on any one point; they would have to look several ways at once'. The plan saw the battalion divided up into separate special parties. At 0020 hours men of 22nd Independent Parachute Company, the pathfinders, would drop on and mark DZ V whilst C Company of 1st Canadian Para followed to defend it. The main battalion drop was to be at 0050 hours; a rendezvous party would be waiting to organise the men as they congregated in their companies at the edge of the DZ. Meanwhile, a battery reconnaissance party, known as Troubridge party, consisting of Major George Smith and two NCOs, Dusty Miller and Bill Harrold, was to move off to the battery immediately on landing and, having awaited the bombing of the battery by bombers at 0030 hours, work out the best approach to the battery, examine the condition of its defences and assess the enemy's deployments. When the main drop arrived, a taping party, using specialist equipment which was to land with the battalion in a glider, was to head for the battery and begin clearing and taping three lanes through the minefield up to the inner wire.

BATTLEFIELD TOURS

The large and rather attractive château close to Varaville and the eastern edge of DZ V that was used as a German headquarters. It was the job of C Company, 1st Canadian Para Battalion, to neutralise this threat to the DZ. In the event it took considerably longer to achieve this objective than anticipated but it was overwhelmed by 1030 hours. *(Author)*

After 90 minutes Otway would move off from the rendezvous, receive a briefing from Troubridge party in Gonneville, create a 'firm base' as a rallying point on the road on the east side of the battery and, having sent a diversionary party off to cause chaos at the main gates of the battery to the north, launch the main assault between 0410 hours and 0420 hours. The assault would be launched on the arrival of three gliders carrying a *coup de main* force of 56 men and eight sappers commanded by Captain Robert Gordon-Brown (and thus known as G-B Force), which was to land inside the battery. As these gliders landed, B Company was to breach the inner wire in three places with Bangalore torpedoes, allowing C Company to attack the casemates. A Company would be in reserve ready to mop up. The guns were to be neutralised by the sappers and success was to be signalled by red-green-red 2-inch mortar flares. Navy signallers attached to the battalion would also send a success signal to the cruiser *Arethusa*, which had been ordered to open fire on the battery if it had not received any such signal by 0530 hours. Meanwhile, the battalion would return to the firm base and then move off to its next rendezvous at the Calvary to the south of the battery.

The plan was complicated, some have argued overly so, but Otway had little choice with the resources that had been made available to him and he had at least ensured that it was a plan that could be modified if things went wrong. In order to anticipate the unexpected, the battalion attacked a full-scale mock-up of the battery, built near Newbury, nine times in May during which various scenarios were played out. By the time that the men of 9 Para reached their transit camp near RAF Broadwell later that month, they were thoroughly prepared for the mission they had to carry out.

Stand B1: DZ V and the 9 Para Rendezvous

DIRECTIONS: Leave Caen and cross the Orne to the east by the main N413 (A-13) road. At the major junction on the outskirts of the city join the N513 heading north. Follow this road (which becomes the D513) past Colombelles and Hérouvillette towards Varaville. After about 6 km from Hérouvillette and just after a lay-by (but before the château) turn left. This château was the one attacked by 1st Canadian Para on the morning of 6 June. This lane bisects DZ V – continue on it for 1 km until it dog legs left where a track turns off to the right. Stop at this junction. Approximately 200 metres to the right by a hedge on the right was the 9 Para rendezvous. Varaville is approximately 1.25 km to the east; Gonneville 1 km to the north-west; the coast is 4 km to the north; and the Merville battery 2 km to the north-west.

THE ACTION: The moment eventually arrived when the battalion was ordered to emplane and at 2230 hours on 5 June, the rendezvous and Troubridge parties boarded their Albemarles at RAF Harwell. Shortly after, the main body of the battalion clambered aboard their Dakotas at RAF Broadwell. G-B Force, meanwhile, waited expectantly at RAF Brize Norton. The pathfinders, rendezvous party and Troubridge party were the first to jump at just 0017 hours.

> **Major George Smith recalled:**
> 'It was a perfect descent. We were not being fired on, although tracer could still be seen firing an arc further and further away, apparently still at the aircraft... I hit the

ground with a hard thud, rolling over onto my back in a manner which would have made the parachute instructors of the Parachute Training School weep with shame.'
Source: Neil Barber, *The Day the Devils Dropped In.*

Smith and his colleagues in the Troubridge party dropped close together and, whilst the pathfinders and the rendezvous party went about their business, moved off towards the battery. As they did so, at around 0030 hours, the Lancaster bombers appeared overhead. Unfortunately, their bombs missed the battery and landed perilously close to Smith, Harrold and Miller. After the ten-minute raid was over, the men continued their journey to the battery across open ground and through ditches so as to avoid any German patrols on the roads and tracks.

The track leading to the 9 Para rendezvous which was in the vicinity of this hedgerow. DZ V spreads out to the east on the other side of the trees on the right. *(Author)*

The rendezvous party, meanwhile, came together slowly to set up the company rallying points but they had completed their task by 0045 hours when they heard the approach of the main lift. The drop, however, was badly scattered as the pathfinders' Eureka beacons had been broken on landing and German flak pushed many aircraft off course. The pathfinders did set up lights on the DZ as a safeguard, but there was just 60 seconds for the pilots to spot those lights once they had crossed the coast, which was virtually impossible after smoke and dust thrown up by the bombers had been blown across the DZ on a westerly wind.

Generalleutnant Josef Reichert, commander of 711th Infantry Division, relates his memory of the night of 5–6 June, as seen from his HQ in Trouville:

'It was a full-moon night and the weather was fairly stormy, with low-hanging black clouds, between which several low-flying planes could be distinctly observed, flying no particular course but moving in a circle around the divisional command post... I heard cries outside of: "Parachutists!" Dashing again into the open, I still saw a few parachutes landing near the divisional command post. In the meantime, the 20-mm anti-aircraft guns which were employed in the strongpoint had opened fire.'

Source: David C. Isby, *Fighting The Invasion*.

When Otway arrived at the rendezvous (a solitary tree in a hedgerow on the western edge of the DZ) at 0130 hours, he was met by Major Eddie Charlton (second-in-command of 9 Para) and the true nature of the dispersal began to dawn on them. As they waited for their comrades, Otway immediately began to revise the plan in his mind to take account of his limited resources – and then he had to revise it again when it became clear that all of the gliders with his special equipment had failed to turn up. Thus, the battalion was without: its 6-pounder guns, signalling equipment, mine detectors, tape, charges to destroy the guns, jeeps and trailers, all but one bundle of Bangalore torpedoes, mortars, all but one Vickers machine gun, and the Navy signallers.

Meanwhile, Troubridge party had crawled along a ditch beside a track heading west from the northern outskirts of Gonneville and reached the junction opposite 'Wood One' with the road (the modern D223) that led south to the Calvary and north alongside the western perimeter of the battery and 'Wood Two'. Harrold was left at this junction to keep watch and to report to the battalion if any accident befell Smith and Miller who then turned right up the lane. As they approached Wood Two they found the track that they were looking for, which led west directly into the battery. It was at this junction, in the south-eastern corner of the wood, that the men cut the perimeter wire and entered the wood and the minefield. The two men kept 30 metres apart for safety and shuffled forward on their hands and knees in order to clear a path for themselves to the inner wire. They eventually got to the western edge of the wood, where there was another cattle fence, which they cut, and then crossed the last 100 metres to the battery in the open. Smith and Miller lay still on reaching the inner wire but heard nothing inside the battery that made their task of assessing deployments and defences any easier. Then, having crawled along the wire to assess any weak points, they met up again and decided that the three best places to breach the wire were on the track, about 70 metres to the right of the track by a telegraph pole, and then 70 metres further to the right again.

The lane connecting Gonneville with the D223, looking west. It was along this ditch that the reconnaissance party crawled soon after landing as they made their approach to the battery. To the left of the lane is where Lieutenant Pond's glider crashed (as described in Stand B3) and it was here that Pond's men encountered a German patrol and had a brief fire-fight. (Author)

Smith then decided to break into the battery in order to obtain the information that he required, but sent Miller back to Harrold with the information already obtained. However, just as Smith was cutting the wire, a tug and glider came into view on the right at an altitude of about 250 metres and the Germans in the battery opened up, giving away their strength and positions to him. With this information, he made his way back to the lane and then back to Harrold and Miller. Just as Smith was leaving with

Harrold to rendezvous with Otway at Gonneville, Captain Paul Greenway's taping party arrived. After a brief exchange of information, the taping party was left to do what they could to clear the mines and mark the lanes without any equipment.

The D223 from Bréville to Descanneville from the southern corner of Wood Two (now removed) at the beginning of the 'attack track' into the battery. On this corner the reconnaissance party cut the cattle fence wire and entered the minefield. *(Author)*

Whilst Troubridge party was at the battery, Otway continued to wait at the DZ rendezvous for his men to arrive. By 0235 hours only 110 men of the expected 620 had reached the position. Otway had a difficult decision to make. He needed as many men as possible to have any chance of neutralising the battery, but if he waited much longer, he would give the Germans a chance to organise themselves and, of course, dawn and the bombardment by the *Arethusa* were creeping ever nearer. He waited just 15 more minutes, time that he had secretly built into his plan for just such a situation, and another 40 men arrived. There is little doubt that Otway was going to go ahead with the attack, but five minutes before setting off for the battery he turned to his batman for reassurance:

'I said, "What the hell am I going to do, Wilson?" "Only one thing you can do, Sir, no need to ask me." And he was right. What else could I do? If I gave up I wouldn't be able to face my colleagues again.'
Source: Neil Barber, *The Day the Devils Dropped In.*

As the depleted battalion moved off in single file for the Gonneville rendezvous with the Troubridge party, Otway changed the plan in his head. All that he needed then was good news from Smith for it to be put into action.

The track taken by Otway and his men from the rendezvous on DZ V to their rendezvous with the reconnaissance party in Gonneville, which is just out of shot on the right. *(Author)*

Stand B2: The Gonneville Rendezvous

DIRECTIONS: Continue along the lane, which joins the D95a road and carries on into Gonneville-en-Auge. Turn sharp right immediately after the church. Continue for 500 metres until a crossroads marked as 'Carrefour du 9ème Bataillon' is reached and a memorial to 9 Para.

THE ACTION: Smith was waiting at the Gonneville rendezvous when the battalion arrived and he made his report to Otway about the failure of the bombers to cut the defensive wire and what he had gleaned from his reconnaissance. With information swapped, the battalion moved off from Gonneville at 0400 hours, led by Major Smith, taking the lane heading west from this crossroads towards the battery. Meanwhile, Greenway's taping party cleared narrow lanes through the minefield by the battery as best they could and tried to mark them by dragging their boot heels or shovels in the dirt and by leaving men to stand by the entrances to the lanes.

The 9 Para Memorial in Gonneville commemorating the final leg of the approach by 9 Para to the battery. It was here that Smith briefed Otway on his findings about the battery's defences. *(Author)*

Stand B3: The Lane

DIRECTIONS: Take the lane heading west (left) from the junction towards the D223. Stop after 200 metres where the hedge ends on the right. It was along this lane that the Troubridge and taping parties moved on their way to the battery and the main body of 9 Para also took this route on leaving the Gonneville rendezvous. However, little happened on the lane until the arrival of the G-B Force just before the assault on the battery was put in (*see Stand 4*) when glider No. 27 of G-B Force landed in an orchard just to the south (left) of this lane. The orchard is no longer there, but a few trees from it remain.

THE ACTION: The second glider of G-B Force, No. 27, carrying Lieutenant Hugh Pond's platoon, had great difficulty locating the battery. Under fire from flak and tracer rounds, the tug circled six times before the glider pilot, Staff Sergeant 'Dickie'

Looking south from the lane connecting Gonneville with the D223. Lieutenant Pond's glider crashed through this hedgerow just as Otway launched the attack on the battery. *(Author)*

Kerr, released from 6,000 feet (1,800 metres) after a pre-arranged signal of a triangle of lights was spotted. Kerr flew a circuit to decrease altitude, being fired upon as he did so (the glider was hit eight times in the fuselage by tracer and twice by cannon; one round knocked it severely off course and caused casualties). The glider passed over the casemates and landed in an orchard some 500 metres from the battery facing south-west, some 20 metres from the lane, with the tail section broken off, the right side torn away and the wings destroyed. The men came out of the aircraft dazed but deployed facing east on either side of the lane when they heard a German patrol approaching. As Pond's platoon opened up, the Germans scattered and the two groups fought at close quarters before the Germans withdrew, hurling abuse at Pond's men. The platoon had not landed where it was meant to, but had proved valuable nonetheless in stopping a German patrol from blundering upon the assault on the battery from the rear.

Earlier, however, Major Smith had led the battalion to the end of the lane from Gonneville to the road junction by Wood One where Harrold and the members of the taping party were waiting. The junction was immediately made into a strongpoint and Otway called an Orders Group to share his revised plan with his company commanders. He was brief and to the point and within minutes the battalion was told what their part in the revised plan was. Otway's calm was impressive; indeed Smith later recalled that he, 'set a fine example which was followed by all ranks. His thoroughness in training paid a fine dividend, the troops were on their toes and ready for the job.' The battalion then headed up the lane towards Wood Two and began to deploy for the assault.

The lane taken by 9 Para, led by Major Smith, from Gonneville to the battery. *(Author)*

Stand B4: The 'Attack Track'

DIRECTIONS: Continue along the lane until the junction with the D223 is reached (Wood One no longer exists). Turn right onto the D223 and continue up the road for 50 m until a track is reached on the left heading west into the Merville battery. Wood Two would have been on the northern side of this track but has also been felled. Note that access to the battery cannot be obtained from this track and, as parking is extremely difficult here, it is advisable to continue to the Merville battery car park (*see Stand 5*) and walk back to this point or to view the track from inside the battery.

The junction of the lane from Gonneville with the D223, looking north-west. The battery is towards the water tower which can be seen in the middle left of the photograph and the track leading from the D223 east into the battery can be distinguished by the line of trees from right to left. *(Author)*

If you have decided to explore the track, walk along it from the D223 towards the battery. After approximately 100 metres stop and look north (right). This is where Wood Two would have ended, and between this point and the battery was open ground. Continue another 100 metres. Just to the north is where the left hand breach was made. The right hand breach was made 70 metres further north.

THE ACTION: The revised plan was for two groups of 15 men of B Company to create just two breaches in the inner wire and for a combined assault party consisting of A and C Companies to be split into four groups of 12 men. The assault was to be led by Major Alan Parry (who was to attack Casemate No. 1 with his own group). As there were no sappers or special charges, the groups would have to do what they could to neutralise the guns and the remainder of the battalion was to be held by Otway for mopping up. There were no working Eurekas, no flares and no mortars and so G-B Force would have to do the best that it could without assistance from the ground save for some coloured lights.

The diversionary party was not dispensed with; indeed it became more important owing to the weaknesses of the battalion, and Sergeant Sid Knight led a slimmed-down version in Lieutenant Brian Browne's absence. As Knight's party moved into position, ten German machine guns opened up – four from inside the battery and three outside from each flank. Otway ordered the single Vickers to knock out those on the left, which it did (helped by the Germans firing tracer) and told Knight's party to silence those on the right. Knight and his team set off with their one Bren gun. They moved north up the road, and knocked out a machine gun at the junction with tracks heading east and west 300 metres up the road. At this junction they took the track on their left heading west which took them towards the main gate. The diversion had begun and the rest of the battalion took up their positions.

Looking west across the D223 along the track to the main entrance to the battery. On the near left corner was the machine-gun nest knocked out by Sergeant Knight and his diversionary party which then followed the track opposite to the main entrance. *(Author)*

The breaching parties made their way along the cleared routes through the minefields, placed their Bangalore torpedoes under the wire, and left one man to detonate them, with the rest retiring a short distance. The assault parties followed them and waited on the lanes behind, just 50 metres from the inner wire. The battalion was in position by just before 0420 hours and awaited

An oblique view from the west of a large scale model made of the Merville battery by Army Intelligence. The village of Merville can be seen in the bottom left hand corner, the battery is clearly visible in the centre left with Wood Two just above it and Wood One to its right separated by a field. The lane from Gonneville to the corner of Wood One can be seen emerging from the top of the model just to the right of centre. *(IWM MH24850)*

G-B Force. Major Charlton stayed at the strongpoint with a few men and the medical officer where he set up a first aid post in a shell crater. In just 70 minutes, the *Arethusa* was due to open up on the battery. Meanwhile, a huge amount of noise was being generated by the diversionary party by the main gate; this had the desired effect as the German response was chaotic.

Just before 0230 hours, G-B Force had begun taking off from England: Gordon-Brown's Glider No. 28 first, followed seven minutes later by Pond's No. 27 and then No. 28a carrying Lieutenant Smythe's men. Gordon-Brown's glider was first over the battery and right on time, but with no Eureka signal they flew around four times under heavy fire before the glider cast off only to come down some distance to the east. Pond's glider landed in an orchard some 500 metres to the south-east, as described earlier, and the third glider had to return to England because of technical difficulties. Thus, Parry blew his whistle, the Bangalores exploded and two gaps six metres across were made in the wire. At this Otway shouted, 'Get In! Get In!' It was 0430 hours.

Stand B5: The Casemates

DIRECTIONS: From the end of the lane continue north up the D223 and after about 200 metres a track heads east (to the right). Knight's party neutralised a machine gun on this corner.

On the other side of the road is the track taken by the diversionary party towards the main gate. Continue past this track another 200 metres and turn left onto the lane to Merville. After 400 metres, turn left down the Avenue de la Batterie de Merville. Go into the car park, which is positioned roughly where the main gate to the battery used to be. Between the two flag poles on the grass outside the entrance is a memorial to 9 Para.

Outside Casemate No. 1 is a bronze bust of Lt-Col Otway which was unveiled in 1997. To its right is a small shelter with a tree growing within it. This was the position of a 20-mm AA gun.

Looking north-west from the 'attack track' leading into the Merville battery.
It was here that Wood Two ended and the open ground to the inner wire began.
(Author)

The tree was a telegraph pole in 1944 that has since taken root. On top of Casemate No. 2 are three orientation tables.

Merville Battery

Musée de la Batterie, Avenue de la Batterie de Merville, 14810 Merville-Franceville; tel: +33 (0)2 31 91 47 53. Museum open 1000–1800 Apr–Sept, 1000–1700 second half of Mar and first half Oct, closed remainder of year. Admission charge; parking. The museum can be found in Casemate 1.

THE ACTION: As Otway yelled 'Get In!', supporting fire was unleashed and the assault party got to its feet and ran towards gaps in the wire, yelling at the tops of their voices.

> **Private Frank Delsignore of C Company remembered the moment:**
>
> 'Alan [Jefferson] was the first one up on his feet and led us into the assault. Any fear I had was gone. We were up and running with Alan, firing from the hip as we went in. We knew there were mines in the ground we had to cover.'
>
> *Source:* Neil Barber, *The Day the Devils Dropped In*.

From the right hand breach Major Parry and Lieutenant Jefferson led the attack on Casemate No. 1 and Lieutenant Mike Dowling on No. 2. Through the left hand breach CSM Ross led the party attacking Casemate No. 3 and Colour Sergeant Long against No. 4. A German flare went up almost immediately the attack began and, as the parachutists entered the battery, they came under heavy fire from machine guns, mortars and snipers; both Parry and Jefferson were hit in their legs and a number in the assault party were killed as mines exploded under them.

> **Lieutenant-Colonel Otway later said:**
>
> 'The garrison concentrated everything waist-high on the gaps in the wire, booby traps and mines were going off all over the place, the battle in our rear was going full tilt and fierce hand to hand fighting was taking place inside the Battery.'
>
> *Source:* Neil Barber, *The Day the Devils Dropped In*.

It was a noisy, smoky and confusing period and there is little agreement on exactly what happened in the following 30

The Merville Battery

An aerial photograph of the Merville Battery taken in May 1944. Many bomb craters can be seen littering the area but the RAF was unable to do severe damage to the casemates. The anti-tank defences can be clearly seen on the northern perimeter of the battery and the four casemates are visible with three clustered around the centre of the photograph and the largest, Casemate No. 1, just above. (IWM MH24804)

a. Casemate No. 1
b. Casemate No. 2
c. Casemate No. 3
d. Casemate No. 4
e. Anti-aircraft gun
f. Magazine for a. and b.
g. Magazine for c. and d.
h. Command bunker
i. Guard bunker with 12 beds
j. Guard room
k. Main gate
kk. Anti-tank ditch
m. Right hand breach
n. Left hand breach

1. 9 Para's movement to breaches
2. Diversionary party's route

A view looking south by the entrance to the Merville battery. The thick inner perimeter wire was approximately 20 metres on the other side of the cattle fence, but following the same line. The left hand breach was made in the middle distance. The line of the track from the D223 into the battery can be seen from the line of trees emerging from the left side of the photograph across to the right side. The right hand breach was made just to the left of the tree which dominates the scene. The bust of Otway can just be seen on its white stone base to the left of the flag poles. *(Author)*

minutes. The bomb craters and trenches impeded the progress of the attackers and, whilst some men fought with the defenders at close range, others pressed on to the casemates. It is likely that the casemates on the right of the attackers, Nos. 1 and 2, were reached first as they were closer to the breach and had fewer obstacles in front of them.

When No. 1 was reached the rear doors were found to be open, hand grenades were thrown inside and some Germans came out and surrendered. The attackers then entered the casemate, and sprayed the rooms inside with Sten gun fire as they moved through to clear them in order to make their way to the gun. In common with the guns in the other casemates, the men found a Skoda (Czech) 100-mm leFH 4/19 field gun (with a range of 11,000 metres), not as powerful as the weapons that they were expecting, but certainly sufficient to hit Sword Beach.

The gun was then neutralised by Gammon bombs (Type 82 anti-tank grenades).

Elsewhere in the battery the fighting was face-to-face and bloody – the diversionary party broke through the main gate to join the battle – and before long casualties littered the ground. Nevertheless, Otway moved forward and took up a position by the right hand breach so that he could gauge what was happening, though he tried to keep moving so as to present a more difficult target. Even so a round passed through the back of his smock and his water bottle, but he was uninjured.

The 'attack track' into the heart of the Merville battery looking west. Casemates 1 and 2 can just be seen in the distance on the right. Casemates 3 and 4 are to the left of the track and obscured by trees. (Author)

Lieutenant Dowling was killed by a mortar, but Casemate No. 2 was entered and the gun destroyed by a shell being placed in the breech, another being rammed down the barrel, and the gun then being fired. The gun in No. 3 was neutralised by the removal of parts of its breech block which were then thrown in various directions. The doors of Casemate No. 4 were shut, but the handful of men who managed to reach it shot through the vision slits and put grenades down the air vents, which forced the Germans inside to open the doors and go out. Inside, the attackers found the gun, damaged the elevating gear and placed a Gammon bomb on the breech block.

Casemate 1 (now a museum) looking north into the battery. This photograph was taken from the track just by the site of the magazine for Casemates 1 and 2. *(Author)*

Meanwhile, Otway sent in the battalion reserve to help deal with those Germans who were still fighting and 9 Para began to gain the upper hand. Officers, including Otway, having checked and re-checked that the guns had been successfully neutralised, yellow smoke candles were lit. This was a pre-arranged success signal which, it was hoped, would be spotted by aircraft of the Fleet Air Arm, which were due to arrive over the area 30 minutes after dawn. The time was 0500 hours.

Meanwhile, prisoners (23 in total) and the wounded were being dealt with, under increasing shell and mortar fire from neighbouring German positions which made it impossible to remove some of the badly hurt. Fearing that the *Arethusa* might begin to bombard the battery very shortly and mindful of the fact that the battalion had other objectives to achieve that day, Otway ordered the position to be evacuated.

The 9 Para Memorial by the entrance to the Merville battery. *(Author)*

Stand B6: The Calvary

DIRECTIONS: Retrace your steps to the D223 and turn right (south) towards Bréville, passing the track to the battery and the lane from Gonneville. Stop at the Calvary on the right at the crossroads after about 1,200 metres.

THE ACTION: The battalion drifted to the Calvary rendezvous where the officers and NCOs endeavoured to take stock of their situation. Sergeant Daniels:

'I saw the Colonel sitting on the Calvary, with his head in his hands. He had been through a tremendous amount.

To take what few men he had in to attack that Battery, was beyond human expectancy. What he'd put up with organising the job and then doing it with so few tools, and knowing full well that we had a full day in front of us.'

Source: Neil Barber, *The Day the Devils Dropped In.*

Major Parry arrived in a wheelbarrow sipping whisky from a flask. He made the sombre men smile when he said, 'A jolly good battle, what?' By 0530 hours the remnants of the battalion had all congregated at the Calvary and it was found that only 80 men were still on their feet; a further 22 wounded were ordered 200

1st Special Service Brigade commandos on the afternoon of 6 June having just crossed the bridges over the Caen Canal and the River Orne. Note that the man on the right has a bayonet attached to his Sten gun and the lance-corporal in the foreground has a Browning 9-mm pistol. The berets are worn without a cap badge in action but the men wear the 4 Commando shoulder title in red and white on black and the Combined Operations flash. The man on the left has extra ammunition in a cotton bandolier and extra Bren gun magazines in a special quick release canvas harness. *(IWM B5058)*

metres down the road to a farm that had been designated as a regimental aid post (now a stud farm called Haras de Retz) together with three prisoners, a doctor and two medical orderlies. The remnants of the battalion were then reorganised for the march ahead and moved off for le Plain at 0600 hours.

The village of le Plain/Amfréville (distinguishable by its church tower) at the northern end of the Bavent Ridge. This photograph is taken from the 12 Para rendezvous looking north-east across DZ N. *(Author)*

TOUR C

THE SOUTHERN FLANK

OBJECTIVE: A tour that examines the southern sector of the division's front at Ranville, le Bas de Ranville, the Ring Contour, Longueval and Ste-Honorine during 6–7 June 1944.

DURATION/SUITABILITY: Half a day in a car, a full day if walking. Suitable for cyclists, but not for the disabled.

APPROACH TO BATTLE: The protection of the southern flank from German counter-attacks was critical if 6th Airborne Division was to achieve its aims and secure the left flank of the Allied invasion. The ground in this area was open and dominated

Main picture: Hamilcar gliders of 6th Airlanding Brigade arrive on DZ N on 6 June containing the Tetrarch tanks of the 6th Airborne Division Armoured Reconnaissance Regiment. *(IWM B5198)*

Inset: Troops hitching up a trailer to a jeep which has just been off-loaded from a Horsa glider on DZ N. This glider is probably part of the divisional headquarters lift on the morning of 6 June. *(IWM B5200)*

by some higher land to the south of the vital bridges over the Caen Canal and River Orne. The security of this area was shared between 12 and 13 Para who had little option but to take up defensive positions in the cover provided by the villages of le Bas de Ranville and Ranville which gave them clear fields of fire, but no ground to fall back on. It was critical, therefore, for the paras to defend their positions and, as soon as possible, extend the bridgehead further to the south.

Stand C1: DZ N

DIRECTIONS: Drive to Pegasus Bridge as described in Tour A and continue on the D514 over Horsa Bridge until a roundabout is reached. Take the third exit (signposted D514, Sallenelles) and continue for 1 km until a lay-by adjacent to a quarry. Stop here. The DZ stretches out to the east and wonderful views of the Bavent ridge can be obtained from this position.

THE ACTION: Two sticks of pathfinders from 22nd Independent Parachute Company jumped accurately onto DZ N at 0020 hours on the morning of 6 June, but two aircraft dropped their sticks too far to the east. This meant that those men had to move extremely quickly in order to complete their tasks before the main lift just 30 minutes later. To confuse matters even more, some of the pathfinders allocated to DZ K were dropped on N in error but did not realise the mistake.

The simple 6th Airborne Division Memorial in the Ranville War Cemetery. *(Author)*

The main lift was on time, and at 0050 hours 7, 12 and 13 Para began to land on the DZ. The 12 Para rendezvous was at this stand. The 7 Para rendezvous was on the western end of the DZ 500 metres to the south, and 13 Para's was in the southern sector near le Mariquet. With only six aircraft from the 131 that took off from England being shot down by flak, some 2,026 men were dropped as well as 702 containers (of which approximately 400 were collected). The wind did drift many men

to the east side of the DZ, but this was a relatively minor inconvenience and only 16 per cent of the men had failed to join their units within a few days.

The first to arrive at the 12 Para rendezvous were the CO, Lt-Col Johnny Johnson, the A Company commander, the second-in-command of B Company and the RSM. By 0300 hours only about 30 men from each company had reached the rendezvous but Johnson, recognising the importance of seizing his objectives quickly, moved the battalion off to le Bas de Ranville. Meanwhile, 7 Para

The grave of Lt-Col Johnson, DSO, CO of 12 Para, killed on the front line in Amfréville at the beginning of the attack on Bréville. (Author)

had already set out for Bénouville and le Port and 13 Para for Ranville. A Company of 13 Para stayed behind, however, to help men of 591 Parachute Squadron, RE, clear the anti-glider poles covering the DZ/LZ ready for the arrival of the divisional HQ later that morning and 6th Airlanding Brigade that evening.

Stand C2: Ranville

DIRECTIONS: Retrace your route down the D514 and take the first left onto the D37c (with views across DZ N on the left). Continue until a crossroads is reached and turn left to proceed into Ranville. Take the second right onto the Rue des Airbornes and continue towards the church. Stop near the church – there is plenty of parking. The Ranville War Cemetery can be entered to the left of the church.

THE SITE: This cemetery contains 2,563 burials (including 322 Germans) and holds the remains of most of the men from 6th Airborne Division who died in Normandy. The first of those to die were buried in the churchyard, which contains 48 burials

Base map: IGN 1612OT

(including one German), but as the fatalities mounted, the ground next to the church was used.

Stand C3: le Bas de Ranville

DIRECTIONS: Pass the church on your left as you continue along the Rue des Airbornes and down the hill heading south-west past a battle-ravaged Calvary on the right. Continue down a sunken lane for 250 metres and stop by a track on the left immediately after the exit sign for Ranville. Walk up the track and look left (north) towards the edge of the woods when you reach the field – this was 12 Para's position. Immediately in front of you across the field is the former site of the forward hedge position. To the right the ground rises up towards the Ring Contour. (All these positions are described below.) The trees and hedges have all grown up since 1944, making this a far less open area today than it was during the Battle of Normandy.

THE ACTION: 12 Para arrived in le Bas de Ranville with barely 50 per cent of its men. Their job was to protect the bridges from a counter-attack over the open ground to the south. The battalion was in position by 0400 hours and began to dig in. A Company was deployed just to the east of the Orne River bridge; B Company in the hedges on the southern edge of le Bas de Ranville; and C Company on the rising ground to the south of village. An outpost line under Captain J.A.N. Sim, consisting of a dozen men with two machine guns, a 6-pounder anti-tank gun and a forward observer with a radio link to HMS *Mauritius*, was positioned 300 metres forward of C Company behind a hedgerow where they could survey the open fields southwards. The sort of German response that they and the division feared most was an armoured counter-attack and, as the men dug themselves in, the forward observer registered the guns of HMS *Mauritius* on some likely ground over which such an attack could take place.

Approximately 800 metres in front of the C Company screen in the hedgerow was the high ground known as the Ring Contour. Beyond the crest of this critical tactical feature, which dominated the ground all around and gave excellent observation of the surrounding villages and the bridges, the ground dropped away into a shallow valley before Ste-Honorine was reached approximately 1.25 km from the crest. To the west of the crest was a narrow lane that led to the village of Longueval and between it and the crest was a road skirting Longueval and leading to Colombelles. As the battalion was screened by the ridge from the enemy to the south this was a classic reverse slope position, but the paras could not afford for the enemy to take and hold the Ring Contour as from it they would enjoy excellent observation over the British positions.

Having established themselves in their positions, at around dawn the battalion found itself fighting German patrols. These skirmishes did not last long, but they kept the men of 12 Para on their mettle for they knew that, with every passing hour, an armoured attack was more likely. The German attacks against 12 Para increased in intensity during the mid-morning and also affected neighbouring 13 Para in Ranville and divisional HQ.

> **Gale wrote in his memoirs:**
>
> 'Ranville was fairly quiet until about 11am. It was at that hour that we came in for a mortaring… It quickly became apparent that a properly mounted attack was being developed against us as I had anticipated from the South. This attack was delivered by the 125th Panzergrenadier Regiment with Self Propelled guns and tanks, and was launched against 12th Battalion… By 1pm Ranville was cleared [and] the battle died down.'
>
> Source: R.N. Gale, *With the Sixth Airborne Division in Normandy.*

This brief mention does not do justice to the intensity of the fighting that took place during that morning and early afternoon. Approximately 100 men of 21st Panzer Division's 125th Panzergrenadier Regiment attacked that morning in an attempt to break through to the bridges. As the German divisional commander endeavoured to get his armour released for a major attack, *Major* Hans von Luck's regiment, some of which was billeted in the area, endeavoured to do all that it could to dislodge the airborne forces. 12 Para snipers engaged the Germans at some distance and managed to hit a few, but the men in the hedgerow were told by Captain Sim to hold their fire until the enemy were 50 metres away. However, as Sim was about to bark out his command, the Germans disappeared into some dead

The right hand end of the forward hedgerow position taken up by a party from C Company, 12 Para, in front of le Bas de Ranville. This ground slopes quite steeply up towards the summit of the Ring Contour, which can be seen just above the tree line in the far distance. There are far more trees and hedgerows in the area now than there were in 1944. *(Author)*

ground and two German self-propelled guns from 200th Assault Gun Battalion appeared on the horizon.

The *Mauritius* was called to lend some fire support, but her guns were already engaging another target and so 12 Para had to rely on the guns of 4th Anti-Tank Battery secreted in the woods with one of its 6-pounders in the forward position. As the self-propelled guns halted in the open to orientate themselves, they provided a perfect target for the gun in the hedgerow just 70 metres away. However, as it was about to let fly, its team found that the breech block had been damaged and, therefore, that it would not fire. One of the self-propelled guns then turned on Sim's position as the infantry continued to move towards the canal around the British right flank. C Company opened up on them and continued the engagement even though a self-propelled gun targeted them in turn. Sim fired two Very lights towards the river to call for the battalion mortars to open fire and sent a runner to HQ to underline the urgency of the situation. Nevertheless, in just a few minutes his small party had suffered several casualties. Sim and a few others, thinking that their colleagues were all dead, withdrew back to C Company. Running

The Ring Contour

le Bas de Ranville

le Ho...

He. Lo...

① Forward hedgerow position
② C Company, 12 Para positions
③ 12 Para arrives from DZ N, 0400 hours
④ German attacks, 6 June
a Site of modern factory
b Stand C3
c The Ring Contour
Base map:
GSGS 4347 Ouistreham 40/16NE
Stop Press edition, 20 May 1944

0   100   200
Metres

Fe de

across the 300 metres of open ground to the edge of the woods and into a shallow ditch that led into the main position, Sim made it back just as the battalion mortars hit the hedge.

Still alive and fighting in the forward position, however, were Lance-Corporal Frank Gleeson with a rifle and Private Andrew Gradwell with a Bren. Gleeson and Gradwell were now isolated, pinned down by German machine-gun fire and fired upon from behind by the battalion's mortars. With the German armour just 50 metres away, Gradwell withdrew back to C Company under Gleeson's covering fire. Gleeson decided to take another route back, through a field behind him filled with unharvested corn. He moved right, onto the road, and jumped into a ditch but found it already occupied by six Germans manning an MG 42. He was

A view from the slope leading up to the Ring Contour looking towards le Bas de Ranville. The forward position of 12 Para in the hedgerows was across the field in the middle distance with the main battalion positions at the edge of the woods. Ranville can be seen in the distance with DZ N behind and the Bavent Ridge (Bréville and Amfréville) on the horizon. *(Author)*

immediately taken prisoner and sent to the rear. The self-propelled guns, meanwhile, moved through the hedge but were stopped when both were hit by 6-pounders firing from B Company positions on their left. As the Germans began to withdraw, patrols and snipers were sent out from 12 Para to clear the Germans in front of their positions and another section of C Company went out and reoccupied the hedge.

Stand C4: The Ring Contour

DIRECTIONS: Continue up the lane to the crossroads with the D223. Opposite is a factory (disused in 2003) with some hard standing in front – park there. Behind the buildings of the factory is the summit of the Ring Contour which, for the fit, can be clambered up for magnificent views to the south and east.

Men of 3 Commando digging in during the afternoon of 6 June on the southern edge of DZ N. These men were to play an important role in counter-attacking the Germans attacking from Ste-Honorine just a few hours later. *(IWM B5051)*

THE ACTION: The British forces hit back in the early evening with a counter-attack after Germans had again been spotted on the Ring Contour. A Troop from the newly arrived 3 Commando of 1st Special Service Brigade moved up to the crossroads south of le Bas de Ranville where it was joined by A Company of 7 Para. The attack began at 1900 hours and was supported by the artillery of 3rd Infantry Division from across the river. The aim was to take the Ring Contour and hold it for as long as possible. A Company was initially forced back but the attack was eventually successful. At around 2100 hours the battle died down, just as 6th Airlanding Brigade began to land on LZ N. For a time the position of 12 Para had been precarious, but the fact that they managed to push the Germans away was good for their confidence and gave them a vital insight into what to expect when, as they anticipated, the enemy attacked again.

> *Major* Hans von Luck, commanding 125th Panzergrenadier Regiment, talking about the end of the first day of the invasion:
>
> '[It was]... clear to the last man that the invasion had succeeded, that it could now be only a matter of days or weeks before the Allies would have landed sufficient forces to be able to mount an attack on Paris, and finally on the German Reich. If it were not for that damned air superiority... The air attacks never stopped; the navy laid a barrage of fire on our positions... By day it was even worse; at any movement on the battlefield, even of an individual vehicle, the enemy reacted with concentrated fire from the navy or attack by fighter-bombers.'
>
> *Source:* Hans von Luck, *Panzer Commander*.

Stand C5: Longueval

DIRECTIONS: Turn onto the D223 heading south-west away from Ranville. Continue 500 metres to the D223/D223a junction – a red and white striped chimney emerges from a factory on the other side of the road. Turn left here and then take the first right and continue into Longueval. As you drive into the village, the route taken by 1 RUR into Longueval (in the dead-ground towards the Orne) can be seen on the right. Approximately 500 metres further on the right is a memorial to 1 RUR. About 600 metres after entering Longueval a major track makes a junction with the road on the left; this track follows the 1 RUR line of advance towards Ste-Honorine. This track is unmade and should only be attempted by car in dry weather. If the conditions are suitable, drive along the track, noting the large conurbation which can be seen some distance ahead to the front right – this is Cuverville. Ste-Honorine is straight ahead in a slight depression and partly hidden by trees. On reaching a crossroads (junction with the D223), go straight across onto a narrow lane until another crossroads is reached (junction with the D513) and go straight over again to enter Ste-Honorine. Stop where possible to look back towards Longueval.

If the track cannot be used because of poor conditions, continue through Longueval and Colombelles and take a left turn onto the D226a. At the roundabout after 1 km take the exit signed D513 Hérouvillette and then take the second right towards Ste-Honorine to rejoin the route given above.

A view looking south from the Ring Contour. Immediately its tactical importance can be seen, with wonderful views towards Longueval (now mainly obscured by trees), Colombelles and Caen in the distance. Views such as this were available in all directions in 1944. *(Author)*

THE ACTION: By the morning of 7 June, 6th Airlanding Brigade had arrived and was ready to strike out southwards and extend the bridgehead to provide a greater buffer zone between the British positions and the bridges. 2 OBLI had moved into concealed positions in Ranville and le Bas de Ranville in readiness for their attack on Escoville. C Company, 1 RUR, had taken up positions on the Ring Contour whilst the rest of the battalion in le Bas de Ranville prepared for their attack on Longueval. At 0900 hours, the main body of the Ulster Rifles set off along the east bank of the Orne towards Longueval with B Company on the right and A Company on the left, covered by C Company on the Ring Contour and D Company in reserve.

Only the battalion's own mortar support was available for this attack, however, and it was therefore fortunate that the village was found to be undefended.

The I RUR memorial in Longueval. (Author)

As A, B and D Companies were digging in at Longueval that morning, however, the less fortunate C Company, which was in full view of the Germans in Ste-Honorine 1.25 km away, was targeted by gun and mortar fire by 200th Assault Gun Battalion and units of 125th Panzergrenadier Regiment. With the company under heavy fire and suffering casualties, the 1 RUR CO, Lt-Col Jack Carson, decided that he had to take Ste-Honorine as soon as possible.

Stand C6: Sainte-Honorine

DIRECTIONS: Continue on the narrow lane into Ste-Honorine, noticing the stout buildings and wall to the right which formed part of the defences of the village. It was from this area that the Germans sent patrols and launched their counter-attacks towards Longueval. Turn left at the church and then bear left after 180 metres to reach a junction with the D513. The Germans moved up the track opposite in open order to the Ring Contour just after 1500 hours on 7 June, and then on towards A Company, 12 Para, dug in on the southern outskirts of le Bas de Ranville.

THE ACTION: Carson's plan to take Ste-Honorine was for one company to hold on to Longueval and two companies to attack the village at 1100 hours. Fire support would come from C Company on the Ring Contour which was to lay down fire on the village with mortars for 15 minutes before the attack, and 3rd Division guns which were to support the attack by bombarding Ste-Honorine from three minutes before H-Hour to two minutes past. In the event, although the fire support plan went ahead as planned, the two attacking companies did not

BATTLEFIELD TOURS

advance at 1100 hours as they had taken too long to move up to the line of departure. Unbeknown to those supporting his attack due to communications difficulties, Carson had postponed the attack until 1215 hours. The problem, however, was that not only had surprise been lost, but the Ring Contour party did not have enough ammunition for a second bombardment of the village. The 3rd Division artillery was also required elsewhere and, worryingly, at 1210 hours seven German self-propelled guns were spotted moving to the village from Escoville.

A view looking south-east out of Longueval. It was across these fields in the same direction as the track that 1 RUR attacked Ste-Honorine unsuccessfully on 7 June. Ste-Honorine is masked by the trees and is behind the white buildings in the centre of the photograph in a depression. The attacking troops would undoubtedly have made good targets for the waiting Germans in the village as they would have been silhouetted against the skyline as they made their final approach. *(Author)*

Again, communication difficulties meant that Carson did not receive this intelligence in time and so 1 RUR moved forward without the crucial information and with only smoke covering their advance over the open fields. The result was that, although some lead elements of A and B Companies managed to enter Ste-Honorine (led by Majors Gerald Rickord and Charles Vickery), they had a difficult fight with the Panzergrenadiers there and were soon forced to withdraw. The British casualties were seven officers and five men dead and four officers and 64 men wounded. A further officer and 67 men were reported as missing, but 20 of these returned on the following day.

Carson therefore had to consolidate in Longueval and his C Company was forced to leave the Ring Contour owing to the weight of fire on it – the company's losses were one officer and 20 men wounded. The attack had been extremely badly handled, particularly as fire support was weak and surprise had been lost and there were no resources with which to follow up the initial break-in to the village. However, communications difficulties had an important impact, as did the tenacity of the German defenders.

These events encouraged the Germans in Ste-Honorine and at 1500 hours they sent a company of infantry forward, supported by four tanks, up the track to the Ring Contour. As the German infantry and tanks appeared atop the Ring Contour, 12 Para opened up with rifles and Brens. The crew of one 6-pounder lost their nerve and ran away, but Private Hall of 3 Platoon manned it himself and knocked out two tanks. The third was hit by 17-pounder fire from the B Company area. The Germans and their one remaining tank then withdrew back to Ste-Honorine. At 1800 hours 12 Para was relieved in le Bas de Ranville by 12th Devons who had arrived by sea that morning and were twice the strength of 12 Para. They dug-in in the hedges and trees on the southern edge of the village with two companies in reserve.

Generalleutnant **Edgar Feuchtinger, commander of 21st Panzer Division, on the events of 7 June:**

'The 125th Panzergrenadier Regimental Combat Team was involved in heavy fighting with the 6th British Airborne Division. Particular difficulties were attached to regrouping 2nd Battalion, 125th Panzergrenadier Regiment, which, partly surrounded, had been fighting since the early hours of the morning. [The enemy] was trying to extend his bridgehead in order to gain the important heights near Ste-Honorine, while on the other hand Combat Team 125 was trying to narrow down this bridgehead. Already at this early date the enemy's superior weight in men and matériel became obvious.'

Source: David C. Isby, *Fighting In Normandy – The German Army From D-Day to Villers-Bocage.*

TOUR D

THE BATTLE OF BRÉVILLE

OBJECTIVE: A tour examining the assembly of 12 Para and D Company, 12th Devons, in Amfréville and their attack on the village of Bréville on the evening of 12 June.

DURATION/SUITABILITY: Half a day. Suitable for cyclists and the disabled.

APPROACH TO BATTLE: The village of Bréville is at the northern end of the Bavent Ridge with commanding views both east and west and was, as a result, a critical piece of high ground. The Germans understood the importance of the area and Rommel had said on one of his inspection visits, 'Whoever holds this ground will control the battle.' As a result, the village was the focus of a good deal of fighting during the first week of the Battle of Normandy, although interestingly it was not until the last few days of that period that the British actually had the resources to try to take and hold it. The reason why Gale was so desirous of Bréville by 10 June was that the village was the one significant gap in his line. The Germans launched attacks from the village against the Commandos at le Plain and Amfréville,

A photograph taken looking north from the southern end of the Amfréville green with its large church. A memorial to the men of No. 6 Commando, who had been fighting in the village for days, is in the foreground. *(Author)*

against 9 Para in the woods at St-Côme, and against Ranville and the bridges. As Gale said, the village was, 'a running sore which had to be lanced.' Thus, there was an attempt to take Bréville from the south by the Black Watch on 11 June, but this failed and a German counter-attack from the village on the following day forced Gale to find the resources for another attack.

This attack was not to take place on the 13th, as might have been expected, but was hurriedly prepared for dusk on the 12th. This was so Gale could use the firepower of a squadron of Sherman tanks from 13th/18th Hussars and the 100 guns from four field regiments and one medium regiment that were only available to him until midnight. Gale also hoped to catch the Germans cold, for he knew that the 346th Infantry Division had lost most of its 857th Grenadier Regiment two days before and believed that the Bréville garrison would be extremely tired, having been fighting all day in the St-Côme woods. In order for surprise to be achieved, however, speed was vital and so planning was kept to a minimum. There was little or no time for reconnaissance and the troops required had to move quickly if they were to reach the line of departure in time. The problem was exacerbated by the fact that the troops that 6th Airborne Division had available for the attack were some way from their start line. The remaining 9 officers and 350 men of 12 Para were in reserve at the quarry by the Orne, and the 6 officers and 80

The quarry where 12 Para was held in reserve and from which the battalion set out towards le Plain. *(Author)*

men of D Company, 12th Devons, had been preparing to support an attack against Ste-Honorine at 0400 hours the next morning from le Bas de Ranville.

Lt-Col Johnson of 12 Para received his orders personally from Gale at divisional HQ at 1900 hours and was told that the attack would be launched from the southern edge of Amfréville (held by 6 Commando). The forming-up line was to be on a lane leading down the western edge of the wood and orchards which covered much of the ground between Amfréville and Bréville, and the line of departure was at the eastern edge of the wood. H-Hour was to be 2200 and, Johnson was told, he would have D Company, 12th Devons, and a squadron of 13th/18th Hussars tanks under command for the attack. There would be a short preliminary artillery bombardment by 53rd Light Regiment on Bréville. The guns were then to fire concentrations on the near fringes of the village and on the south-eastern and south-western exits from H-10 minutes to H-Hour, before lifting their fire to the rear part of the village from H-Hour to H+10. By the time that Johnson had been briefed it was 1930 hours and he returned to his battalion, warned them to prepare for battle and briefed his company commanders. The battalion was to head for Amfréville, where they were to gather in the church. Here they would receive more detailed orders from the company commanders by 2130 hours.

Stand D1: The Route to Amfréville

DIRECTIONS: Follow the directions in Tour B, Stand 1, to the quarry beside the D514 north of Ranville. This had been the 12 Para rendezvous on D Day and was also the place where they were held in divisional reserve on 12 June. From here continue north up the D514 for 1 km until a sign on the right is reached for Amfréville – but take the road on the left towards the Orne which is signposted as a dead end. Continue to the end (where you can turn your car) where there is a cluster of houses – la Basse Écarde. Looking south with the Orne on your right, a track can be seen and it was up this track through the hamlet that 12 Para and the Devons marched on their way to Amfréville.

THE ACTION: With no time to spare, Johnson collected his company commanders and took them off in a jeep to conduct a reconnaissance of the ground. Having left the battalion at the quarry, they visited 6 Commando's HQ in a farm on the road a couple of hundred metres to the east of Amfréville and then walked forward through two orchards to a hedge where the forward sections of the commando were dug in. From here they scanned the open fields to Bréville, some 400 metres away. The Germans held the houses to the right of the hedge along the main road from Amfréville to Bréville and were known to have infantry and self-propelled guns in the village. Two Black Watch carriers, which had been destroyed in the abortive attack of the previous day, could be seen on the road.

Johnson fine-tuned the plan that he already had in mind and explained it to his company commanders, except for Major John Bampfylde of the 12th Devons who had not yet arrived. The plan was for an attack on a single-company front along the line of the road leading into Bréville. C Company, commanded by Major C.W. Stephens and comprised of three weak platoons of about

A view looking south along the track near the Orne that 12 Para and the Devons took on their way to le Plain. *(Author)*

15 men each, was to lead and seize the crossroads at the southern end of Bréville and the houses to the left of it. A Company, commanded by Captain P.C. Bernhard, was to follow and take the small château at the eastern corner of the village. D Company of 12th Devons was to attack in the next wave and was to enter Bréville, swing left and then seize the orchard in the north-east corner of the village. B Company, under Major H.D. Rogers, was then to occupy the western edge of the village. The tanks, meanwhile, were to put one troop along the road on the right of the attack in order to shoot up the houses between Amfréville and Bréville whilst the rest of the squadron on the left was to target the front edge of the village and protect the left flank.

At 1930 hours, D Company, 12th Devons, was relaxing in an orchard at le Bas de Ranville when Bampfylde received his new orders. Having briefed his second-in-command, Captain John Warwick-Pengelly, Bampfylde rushed off to reconnoitre the ground over which his company was to attack. Meanwhile, as his men were jerked out of their slumbers, Warwick-Pengelly held an 'O' Group for the platoon commanders and the company departed quickly for its 5-km march to Amfréville in the wake of 12 Para. Their route along the narrow and rough path to the east of the Orne was difficult ground to negotiate as it was cut up by slit trenches and craters. In places the path was less than two metres wide and heavily overgrown. For the heavily laden troops, some of whom were dragging hand-carts full of ammunition, it was difficult to maintain the speed that was required for them to reach Amfréville in time for the attack.

As they reached the beginning of the lane into le Plain at around 2045 hours, the company checked to allow the rear platoon to catch up. The men then had to flatten themselves into the hedges, hand-carts and all, to allow a troop of Shermans to go by. Cursing the dust kicked up by the tracks and the inconvenience, the men did at least take comfort that they were to be supported by armour in their attack. Shortly after, Major Eddie Warren, commander of the Devons' support company, turned up in his jeep to watch the attack. Warren hitched two of the hand-carts to his vehicle and ran them up the hill to the relief of their handlers. By this stage the men were almost running in order to get to the concentration area in time. Minutes later they entered le Plain and slowed once again to close up – it was now 2130 hours.

BATTLEFIELD TOURS

The road (a narrow lane in 1944) up which 12 Para and the Devons marched into le Plain. The Devons had to flatten themselves into the hedge to make way for the squadron of Sherman tanks heading for the start line. *(Author)*

Stand D2: le Plain

DIRECTIONS: Retrace your route from la Basse Écarde to the crossroads with the D154 (with the hotel/restaurant *le Derby d'Epsom* on the corner) and go straight across. Continue into le Plain (marked on 1944 maps as le Plein) and turn right at the junction and then first right again to park your car by the *mairie*. The large church in the centre of the green cannot be missed.

THE ACTION: 12 Para left their quarry at 2030 hours and marched to le Plain, where they then filed into the church and sat in the pews ready to receive their orders. The platoon leaders were briefed by their company commanders and then the orders were passed on to the men. The atmosphere was tense; nobody liked to be rushed into an attack particularly when it was a fight divorced from their parent brigade. Nevertheless, once the platoons had been briefed and questions answered, the battalion left the church in the order in which they were due to attack – C Company followed by A Company and then B Company

ongue

R14 H2

le Plein

Amfréville

Bréville

Chau

R14 HBD2

R15 HB D2

R15 HB D2

R8 B2

R15 B2

R15 H2

R8 B2

R12 H2

R15 H2

R8

① Assembly area
② Start line
③ B Company, 12 Para
④ D Company, 12 Devons
⑤ C Company, 12 Para
⑥ A Company, 12 Para

Base map:
GSGS 4347 Ouistreham 40/16NW
Stop Press edition, 20 May 1944

0   100   200
Metres

The church in Amfréville. It was here that the men of 12 Para received their orders and then headed towards the camera's position and into the woods behind the line of departure. *(Author)*

followed by HQ Company – and headed for the forming-up line on a lane leading down the western edge of the wood in Amfréville.

The farm building and courtyard entrance in Amfréville where Major Warren left his jeep and then came across the devastation caused by the shell that wounded Brigadiers Lovat and Kindersley. *(Author)*

Stand D3: Amfréville

DIRECTIONS: Head past the church and at the bottom of the green take the left fork which immediately takes you past the front of an old farm and stop there. Walk down the lane and in the fields on the left can be seen the remains of the wood and orchard from which the attack on Bréville was launched. At the junction at the end of the lane, you can still see the edge of the former wood (the hedge remains) from which 12 Para and the Devons emerged. Bréville church tower can be seen over the top of some new houses that have been built on the battlefield. On the right, however, the Amfréville–Bréville road can be seen with its original houses which were held by German troops.

THE ACTION: 12 Para approached the start line just as the guns opened fire at 2150 hours, but its platoon commanders were still reconnoitring the ground over which they were to advance. Bampfylde had only just found the 12 Para CO and had not contacted his own company which, without precise orders, was at this time mixed up with the men from 12 Para in le Plain. Warren tried to find Bampfylde and left his jeep and driver at a farmhouse. By this time the Germans were slamming shells into Amfréville. As Warren crossed the farmyard he saw the aftermath of a shell which had torn into a group including Kindersley and Lovat and wounded both badly. Warren continued on and then almost came to a halt as he ran into a log-jam of paras moving forward to the start line. There was much confusion, and the smoke fired as part of the bombardment blowing back onto the troops did not help. Warren looked for Bampfylde and eventually found him by the start line, very harassed and fearing that his men would go into battle without the information they needed.

Bampfylde sent Warren back to hurry the company on and, as Warren was pushing his way back through the paratroopers, German shells fell on the orchard causing heavy casualties among 12 Para's A and C Companies.

> **Captain Gordon Medds remembers:**
> '... as we entered the wood, things began to hot up. Shells started exploding in the trees around us, always a disconcerting experience as the trees seem to magnify the sound alarmingly.'
> *Source:* Eric Barley and Yves Fohlen, *Para Memories.*

BATTLEFIELD TOURS

Looking towards the village of Bréville from the line of departure just to the south of Amfréville. The housing on the left is new and now occupies a large proportion of 1944's no-man's-land. The house on the right is original and is on the Amfréville–Bréville Road. *(Author)*

The CO of 12 Para, Lt-Col Johnson, his second-in-command, his adjutant, the RSM and Bampfylde were all killed. The attack began just minutes later whilst Warren was dazed and struggling to make sense of a confusing scene. C Company advanced in scenes reminiscent of the Somme battlefield. Medds has said:

'We all stepped out of the wood and into the open ground, our weapons drawn, bayonets fixed, to start the assault on Bréville which we could now see for the first time about 200 metres away. Almost as though the sight of us stepping forward was a signal, what had been fairly sporadic fire until then escalated suddenly, and the whole field ahead of us started to erupt. The air was full of the noise of small arms fire from Bréville and from our flanking tanks, the thump of German 88-mm self-propelled guns, and worst of all, I fear, the deafening crack/crump of our own artillery... The sound and fury of the barrage of fire that was destroying us all made it difficult to think clearly – indeed to think at all. So much so that when after about 100 metres of advancing like automatons I felt something like a warm smooth broom handle being pushed through my right leg, it didn't occur to me that I had been hit, although it did unbalance me and I stumbled to my knees.'

Source: Eric Barley and Yves Fohlen, *Para Memories*.

Almost immediately C Company lost both its officers and its CSM and found no cover until just 15 men reached the outskirts of Bréville, led by Sergeant Warcup. A Company followed across the open ground and, as its men entered Bréville, a self-propelled gun opened fire and killed CSM Marchwood who was leading after Captain Bernhard had been wounded at the start line.

By the time that the bulk of the Devons had arrived at the start line, the lane was choked with men from B Company of 12 Para and the wounded from A and C Companies. In this desperate situation, the Devons attacked in dribs and drabs with some men from B Company mixed up with them. Some were led through the hedge by Warren and others by Warwick-Pengelly. This mixed force had little difficulty crossing the 300 metres or so of open ground as the shelling had ceased. The Shermans on the left also broke cover to engage the enemy's forward positions whilst those on the right moved up the Bréville road and shelled the houses.

The lane beside the farm which led to the woods and the front line. This lane was full of wounded from 12 Para when the Devons reached it. *(Author)*

A ragged B Company followed the Devons, led by Colonel Reggie Parker, deputy commander of the Airlanding Brigade and a former CO of 12 Para. Having learned of Johnson's death, Parker had come forward with some stragglers in order to establish a command post in Bréville and organise the defence of the village. B Company also reached Bréville with very little opposition and took up defensive positions in the orchard near the church, which was criss-crossed by German trenches filled with their dead. Although often light in manpower, the attacking companies attained their objectives. The troop of Shermans on the right of the attack advanced to the crossroads and the tanks on the left moved to the north-east outskirts of the village.

Stand D4: Bréville

DIRECTIONS: Turn left onto the Amfréville–Bréville Road and continue into Bréville; park near the church. The remains of the

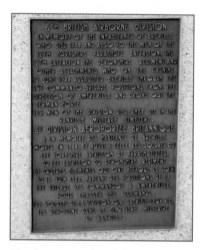

original church can be seen in the churchyard and a little further on is the important Bréville crossroads which has remarkable views to the south.

The Bréville crossroads memorial to 12 Para and the Devons. *(Author)*

THE ACTION: On reaching Bréville, Parker moved forward to reconnoitre the village and assess the situation, but the fighting continued all around as the British troops endeavoured to flush out the remaining Germans. By the time that Parker went on his tour it was 2245 hours: a few men of C Company, 12 Para, under Sergeant Warcup held the crossroads

The Amfréville–Bréville Road with the Bréville church in the background. The original house on the right was full of Germans on 12 June and it was up this road that a troop of Shermans advanced in support of the attack. *(Author)*

A Sherman tank from the 13th/18th Hussars moves through the fields on the outskirts of Bréville. The destruction wrought by the British guns on the village the previous evening can clearly be seen in the background. *(IWM B5471)*

beyond the church; A Company was around the château with Sergeants Nutley and Murray and 18 men; 20 of the Devons were in the orchard in the north-east corner of the village (later supplemented by stragglers taking their strength to 75 men); and B Company held the west side of the village. As Parker moved around, an intense concentration of British artillery fire hit the village. There are various theories as to why this occurred: it is possible that the code words for the pre assault fire plan and that for the consolidation or any necessary counter-attack – Acorn One and Acorn Two – were too similar and easily misheard on the radio during a battle, but it has also been said that two white Very lights were fired from near the château just before the bombardment began and that they could well have been taken as a signal for a renewed bombardment. Whatever the cause, the guns caused heavy British casualties but also finally ended the last vestiges of German resistance in Bréville and allowed the new defenders of the village to consolidate their gains.

Corporal Ron Dixon, Signals Platoon, 12 Para, who attacked with C Company against Bréville on 12 June:

'I went into the attack carrying on my back a No. 68 radio set. I was with the advance company crossing the open fields into Bréville. It was as though hell had been let loose

The rebuilt Bréville church with the remains of the original, which was destroyed in the battle. Men from 12 Para endeavoured to dig-in in this area amidst wailing sounds that some believed were emanating from the church organ pipes. *(Author)*

– mortars, shells, airbursts, machine guns all firing at once. There was no cover until we got to the village itself. "Take cover!" I heard called. I saw a slit trench and dived in and landed on top of a bloke who I thought was one of our lads until he spoke. "Prisoner," he said, "Prisoner," and handed me a Luger. I was speechless, I then heard, "Attack! Attack!" I said to the Jerry. "Sorry chum, you stay here." I got out of the slit trench and followed a sergeant and a number of our lads to the houses in Bréville. A number of us were sheltering against a wall of a château when a shell or mortar bomb dropped among us, killing three and injuring the remainder. I picked myself up and, to my amazement and relief, found that I hadn't been scratched…'

Source: Eric Barley & Yves Fohlen, *Para Memories.*

When Major Warren met Parker, the colonel was in great pain and half-delirious owing to a wound, but before he was evacuated he managed to persuade the Sherman squadron commander to leave a troop of tanks in support of the men at the crossroads. Meanwhile, 12 Para and the Devons dug in and patrolled, but found only enemy dead and some cowering civilians. As usual, the fear was an early German counter-attack, but none came.

Early on the following day, Major Stockwell and 50 men from the pathfinders arrived to bolster the defences and that afternoon the exhausted attackers were relieved by a combined force of 12th Devons and 1 RUR. Bréville had been taken, but at a cost: 12 Para had lost its commander, 7 more officers and 133 men, whilst D Company, 12th Devons, had lost its commander and 35 soldiers; 78 German bodies were found in the village.

> **The War Diary for the Devons is scathing. It accepts that quick attacks without reconnaissance are sometimes required, but goes on to assert that:**
>
> 'Battle procedure can be speeded up or cut down but cannot be totally eliminated. It is not sufficient for commanders to know the objective etc. as they invariably become casualties. Time is required for all ranks to be advised…'
>
> *Source:* 12 Devons War Diary.

It is difficult to argue with this, though the fog of war was particularly dense on the Bréville battlefield on 12 June, but crucially for 6th Airborne Division and the Allied commanders, the Bréville gap had been closed. The Germans also knew that an important stage had been passed.

The splendid view south from the forward position of 12 Para at the Bréville crossroads across DZ N to Ranville and beyond. *(Author)*

Oberst Paul Frank about 346th Division on 12 June in Bréville:

'In the late evening, after a very heavy half-hour bombardment, the enemy attacked in great force to the east and south of Amfréville, threatening the rear of our forces in the south of Bréville... Having no forces available for counter-attack, division HQ decided to abandon the forward position at Bréville, and to establish a new MLR [main line of resistance] west of the Dives lowland, which would ensure flank support for the coastal defences east of the Orne and could be used to launch further attacks. Thus the first counter-attack had come to an unsuccessful conclusion.'

Source: David C. Isby, *Fighting In Normandy – The German Army From D-Day to Villers-Bocage.*

The village of Bréville on 13 June after it had been seized by the men of 12 Para and 12th Devons. These troops are moving a German anti-tank gun into position during mop-up operations. A dead German lies in the foreground with recently cut twigs and branches covering a trench just to his right. *(IWM B5472)*

PART FOUR

ON YOUR RETURN

FURTHER RESEARCH

Having visited the Orne bridgehead battlefield, you may wish to carry out further research on the actions that took place there and the units involved. There are a number of museums that may provide you with useful information.

These include: the *D-Day Museum and Overlord Embroidery*, Clarence Esplanade, Southsea, PO5 3NT; tel: 023 9282 7261 (ask for the D-Day Museum); email: <enquiries@ddaymuseum.co.uk>; The *Imperial War Museum*, Lambeth Road, London SE1 6HZ; tel: 0207 416 5000; web: <www.iwm.org.uk>; email: <mail@iwm.org.uk>; and *Duxford Imperial War Museum*, Duxford, Cambridgeshire CB2 4QR; email: <duxford@iwm.org.uk>; the *Airborne Forces Museum* in Aldershot; tel: 01252 349619; the *Museum of Army Flying*, Middle Wallop; tel: 01980 674421; the *Oxfordshire and Buckinghamshire Light Infantry Museum*, Oxford; tel: 01865 780128; the *Military Museum of the Devon and Dorset Regiment*, Dorchester; tel: 01305 264066; the *Tank Museum*, Bovington; tel: 01929 405096; *Royal Ulster Rifles Museum*, Belfast; tel: 028 9023 2086; and *Firepower – The New Royal Artillery Experience*, Woolwich, London; tel: 0208 855 7755.

Although the literature on the Pegasus Bridge *coup de main* is plentiful, remarkably few books have been published on the wider activities of 6th British Airborne Division – and even fewer can be recommended. Nevertheless, the following are useful although not all are still in print:

GENERAL

Crookenden, Napier, *Dropzone Normandy: The Story of the American and British Airborne Assault on D-Day 1944*, Ian Allan, 1976.

Ellis, L.F., *Victory in the West*, Volume I, *The Battle of Normandy*, HMSO, 1962.

Otway, T.B.H., *The Second World War 1939–1945 Army, Airborne Forces*, Imperial War Museum, 1990.

Above: The *Mémorial Pegasus* which boasts a fine collection of artefacts from 6th Airborne Division's time in Normandy The material is presented in an attractive fashion and the division's story is clearly told with the aid of a useful film, an extremely helpful relief map and friendly and knowledgeable staff. *(Author)*

Page 185: A Mk VII Tetrarch I tank emerges from a Hamilcar glider during training. *(IWM CH13380)*

ALLIED UNITS

Aggett, W.J.P., *The Bloody Eleventh – History of The Devonshire Regiment*, Volume III, 1915–1969, The Devon and Dorsetshire Regiment, 1995.

Ambrose, Stephen E., *Pegasus Bridge, June 6, 1944*, Touchstone, 1988.

Anon., *By Air To Battle – The Official Account of the British First and Sixth Airborne Divisions*, HMSO, 1945.

Barber, Neil, *The Day the Devils Dropped In – The 9th Parachute Battalion in Normandy – D-Day to D+6, The Merville Battery to the Château St Côme*, Leo Cooper, 2002.

Barley, Eric, and Fohlen, Yves, *Para Memories, 12th Yorkshire Battalion in Europe and the Far East during the Second World War*, Parapress, 1996.

Bernage, Georges, *Red Devils in Normandy: 6th Airborne Division*, Heimdal, 2002.

Harclerode, Peter, *Go To It! The Illustrated History of the 6th Airborne Division*, Caxton Editions, 1990.

Neillands, Robin, *The Raiders: The Army Commandos 1940–46*, Weidenfeld and Nicolson, 1989.

Salmond, J.B., *The History of the 51st Highland Division 1939–1945*, William Blackwood and Sons, 1953.

Shilleto, Carl, *Pegasus Bridge & Merville Battery – British 6th Airborne Division Landings in Normandy, D-Day, 6th June 1944*, Leo Cooper, 1999.

MEMOIRS

Edwards, Denis, *The Devil's Own Luck – Pegasus Bridge to the Baltic*, Leo Cooper, 1999.

Gale, R.N., *With the Sixth Airborne Division in Normandy*, Sampson Low, 1948.

Vaughan, John, *All Spirits*, Merlin Books, 1988.

THE GERMANS

David C. Isby, *Fighting In Normandy – The German Army From D-Day to Villers-Bocage*, Greenhill, 2000.

Isby, David C., (ed.), *Fighting the Invasion – The German Army at D-Day*, Greenhill, 2001.

Perrigault, Jean-Claude, *21. Panzer Division*, Heimdal, 2002.

Von Luck, Hans, *Panzer Commander – The Memoirs of Hans von Luck*, Praeger, 1989.

Primary source documents relating to the planning and execution of operations in the Orne bridgehead can be found at the National Archive (formerly the Public Record Office), Kew, Richmond, Surrey TW9 4DU; tel: 020 8876 3444; fax: 020 8392 5286; email: <enquiry@nationalarchives.gov.uk> web: <www.nationalarchives.gov.uk>. The following are just are a small selection of those that are relevant (with the classification numbers showing where they can be found):

WAR DIARIES

6th Airborne Division *WO 171/425*; 6 Airlanding Brigade *WO 171/591*; 3rd Para Brigade *WO 171/593*; 5th Para Brigade *WO 171/595*; 1st Special Service Brigade *ADM 202/75*; 9 Para *WO 171/1242*; 12 Para *WO 171/1245*; 13 Para *WO 171/1246*; 7 Para *WO 171/1239*; 8 Para *WO 171/1240*; 22 Independent Para Company *WO 171/1249*; 5th Black Watch *WO 171/1266*; 12th Devons *WO 171/1279*; 2 OBLI *WO 171/1357*; 1 RUR *WO 171/1383*.

INDEX